The New GCSE
Religious Studies
Course for Catholic Schools

Component 1 Catholic Christianity

AQA COMPONENT 1

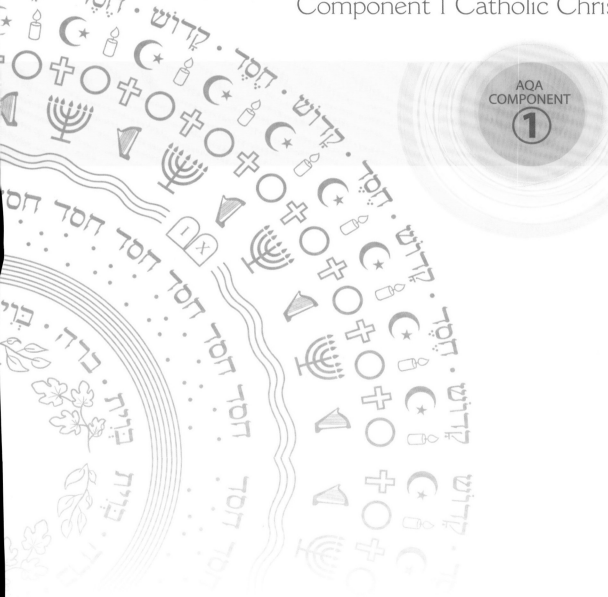

redemptorist
publications

Published by Redemptorist Publications
Alphonsus House, Chawton, Hampshire, GU34 3HQ, UK
Tel. +44 (0)1420 88222, Fax. +44 (0)1420 88805
Email rp@rpbooks.co.uk, www.rpbooks.co.uk

A registered charity limited by guarantee
Registered in England 3261721
Copyright © Redemptorist Publications 2016
First published July 2016

Text by Anthony Towey, Philip Robinson George Skelton, Shelley Victor,
Duncan MacPherson and Ben Gray
Edited by Anthony Towey
Additional contributors: Kathleen O'Brien and Paul Rowan
Designed by Emma Hagan
Cover illustration by Tree Behrens

The image on the cover represents the Covenants, or promises, between God and humankind, many of which are held in common by the Abrahamic Faiths.

The first Covenant is between God and humanity in Adam and Eve. The apple branch refers to the Edenic Covenant which was broken when Adam and Eve ate fruit from the tree of knowledge. The fig leaves represent the curses pronounced when God finds Adam and Eve hiding in the garden wearing fig leaves.

The seven lines refer to the rainbow from the second Covenant, known as the Noahic Covenant. God makes a promise to Noah after the flood never again to submerge the land with water.

The third Covenant is the Abrahamic Covenant. After being tested by God, Abraham is promised descendants as many as the stars (represented by the dots). Abraham means 'father of the people' and he is recognised as a very important figure in Christianity, Islam and Judaism.

The next Covenant is with Moses, who led the Jews out of slavery in Egypt to the Promised Land. On Mount Sinai he received the Law from God, commonly known as the Ten Commandments, or the Law of Moses.

God's Covenant with David refers to land and kingship. God promised that David's kingdom would be established for ever through David's descendants. Christians believe that Jesus is the fulfilment of this promise.

Tree Behrens

Page 11: "Image by Elizabeth Wang, copyright Radiant Light 2016, Image Code: T-03247B-CW".
"From the heart of God has sprung all that exists. Creation is sustained in being by God's power and love. In the very 'heart' of God are held and cherished all who live in His love and who have not utterly and eternally rejected him."

Page 76: "Image by Elizabeth Wang, copyright Christ among his people 2016, Image Code: T-01327-OL".

Nihil obstat: Fr Terry Tastard, Censor
Imprimatur: His Eminence Cardinal Vincent Nichols,
Archbishop of Westminster
13 July 2016

The *Nihil Obstat* and *Imprimatur* are a declaration that a book or pamphlet is considered to be free from doctrinal or moral error. It is not implied that those who have granted the *Nihil Obstat* and *Imprimatur* agree with the contents, opinions or statements expressed.

Redemptorist Publications has used every effort in preparing this guide. It does not assume, and hereby disclaims, any liability to any party for loss or damage caused by errors or omissions in the guide whether such errors or omissions result in negligence, accident or other cause.

You should always check the current requirements of the examination, since these may change. Copies of the AQA specification may be obtained from:

AQA, Stag Hill House, Guilford, Surrey, GU2 7XJ

ISBN 978085231 4579

Printed by Bishops Printers Limited, Portsmouth PO6 1TR

The New GCSE Religious Studies

Course for Catholic Schools

Component 1 Catholic Christianity

AQA
COMPONENT
1

Text by
Anthony Towey
Philip Robinson
George Skelton
Shelley Victor
Duncan MacPherson
Ben Gray

Edited by
Anthony Towey

Additional contributors
Kathleen O'Brien
Paul Rowan

Contents

Online resources available at www.rp-education.co.uk

Introducing Catholic Thinking

[cf. AQA Spec B 3.113]

CORE IDEA

The Three-Legged Stool!

To the surprise of most people, Catholic thinking is not based just on what the **Bible** says, nor just on what **scientists, saints** or **scholars** have said, nor just on what **popes** and **bishops** have said – it is based on a conversation between all three!

'Thinking on a Three-Legged Stool'

Everyone has had the experience of sitting on a wobbly chair or on a stool. It is difficult to get settled and it can be very distracting. Even worse, if one of the legs falls off we can end up on our backside looking pretty daft. There needs to be at least three legs and they need to be strong! The three-legged stool can serve as an image of Catholic thinking about revelation – the way in which God communicates with his people. Although some Christian groups ascribe inspiration only to **the Bible**, Catholics believe that the Bible, the **Tradition** of the Church and its **teaching** authority together provide a sound base for proper thinking about God. Why?

The Bible: Divine Wisdom in Human Words

Just like a normal library, the 'little library' that is the Bible is full of different kinds of writings. There are history books, adventure stories, love stories, battles, poetry, prayer books, hymns, sayings, legends, law books, crime-stoppers, biographies, letters, prophecies and even scary cosmic 'apocalyptic' books. This means there is endless possibility for confusion and we need help to make sense of it all. The first way this has been done is that the Church has gathered the writings into two testaments – two *covenants*. The first is called the 'Old Testament' and it begins with creation and the story of the people of Israel. The second is the 'New Testament' and it begins with the Gospels of Jesus and includes the story of the disciples and the early Church as well as the letters of Paul and other apostles.

KEY TERMS

Scripture Bible = An *inspired* collection of writings sacred to Christians.

Tradition = The *inspired wisdom* captured in the words, customs and lives of Christians.

Magisterium = The *inspired* teaching role entrusted to the Church.

Now it is vital to remember that Catholics do not believe that this collection we call the Bible was discovered already written like the Book of Mormon. It is the opposite. The collection of writings we now call the Bible was deliberately compiled by the Church over many centuries and only completed some four hundred years after the birth of Jesus by Pope Damasus in AD 382. Inevitably, these writings bear the characteristics of the cultures where they were written as well as the thumbprints and smudges of the various scribes who wrote them down, but because they have been considered by the Church to be *inspired* – 'God breathed' (2 Tim 3:16) – the Bible is understood to be both *divine* and *human* because it communicates God's wisdom in our words; it is the way in which 'the invisible God, out of the abundance of His love, speaks to [us] as friends' (*Dei Verbum* 2).

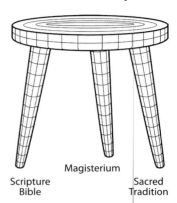

Magisterium

Scripture
Bible

Sacred
Tradition

Tradition: Divine Wisdom in Human Lives

Every family, school, community or gang has sayings, traditions and characteristics specific to them. Catholic Christianity is the same. In the Gospel of John it says that 'not all the things that Jesus did are written down' (John 20:30), and as well as the specific writings in the Bible, there is a broader collection of *inspired* Christian *wisdom* captured in words, customs and lives. This is collectively called *Tradition* and it is the second component of the three-legged stool. In every generation, beginning with the apostles and followers of Jesus, the Holy Spirit helps the Church grow in wisdom through the lives of saints, the writings of theologians and the experience of God's faithful.

Magisterium: Divine Wisdom in Human Teaching

The third element in Catholic thinking can be understood as a collection of inspired *teachings*. In the classroom there will hopefully be lots of debate and a variety of opinions, but eventually the teacher may draw things towards a conclusion or common perspective. 'Magister' is the Latin word for teacher, and 'Magisterium' refers specifically to the inspired role of the Church in the interpretation of scripture and Tradition. This *authority* has been exercised from the earliest times (see Acts 2:42), and it is continued in a particular way by the Pope and the bishops, who are understood to be direct successors of Peter and the apostles. The year 2015 provided two examples of how Magisterium works when the Pope issued a teaching on the environment *(Laudato Si')* and hosted a worldwide discussion among Catholics about the family.

Conscience: Divine Dignity in Human Freedom

Lastly and importantly, while the Church fervently believes the truth of its wisdom, it also teaches the importance of conscience and personal freedom. As *Dignitas Humanae* 11 says, 'God calls men [and women] to serve Him in spirit and in truth, hence they are bound in conscience but they stand under no compulsion. God has regard for the dignity of the human person whom He Himself created and man [woman] is to be guided by his [her] own judgment and he [she] is to enjoy freedom.'

'It is clear, therefore, that sacred tradition, Sacred Scripture and the teaching authority of the Church, in accord with God's most wise design, are so linked and joined together that one cannot stand without the others, and that all together and each in its own way under the action of the one Holy Spirit contribute effectively to the salvation of souls.'

Dei Verbum 10

Discussion

What is your favourite type of book, film or story? Is there anything like it in the 'little library' of the Bible? Can God speak through different types of writing? What *traditions* do you have within your family, at your school, among your friends? Are any of them particularly special or important? Lastly, is it useful to have a recognisable *teaching authority* in the Church – what are the pros and cons? What is the role of conscience?

Summary

Catholic thinking uses three sources of wisdom, and the supreme advantage of this way of engaging with God's revelation is that it sets up a constant dialogue, a permanent conversation *between* the insights of the biblical writers (Scripture), the contemplation and life experience of different generations (Tradition) and the teachings of the Church from the apostles onwards (Magisterium). The Bible itself is an example of this process whereby the gathering and ordering of the writings into a definitive collection took place only after a period of deliberation and contemplation among both ordinary Christians and authorities of the early Church. Among other things, this 'threefold arrangement' makes it impossible for Catholics to be 'fundamentalists' with regard to scripture since the Bible must always be understood thoughtfully, in the light of the tradition and teaching of the whole Church. Finally, with the understanding of the importance of conscience, Catholics should have deep respect for the views and opinions of others and be happy to engage in discussions about human destiny and our role in the world in every context and in every age.

Unit 1A
Creation understood through Art [AQA Spec.B 3.1.1.1]

Creation in Catholic Art: In this unit we explore the Catholic understanding of creation. The notions of God as creator, humanity being formed in the image of God and the call to be good stewards of God's creation we will first explore through art.

Part 1 Michelangelo's *The Creation of Adam*

The Creation of Adam

This picture is from the Sistine Chapel in Rome. Michelangelo (1475–1564) was the most famous of the artists who worked on the chapel, and he had the difficult task of painting the ceiling! He decorated this with nine different scenes – three from the creation of the cosmos, three from the creation of humanity and three from the story of Noah and the Flood. The best-known of these is *The Creation of Adam*, which explains through art a number of things which Christians understand about humanity and God. In the picture, we humans are represented by Adam.

1 **God is the all-powerful Creator – we are creatures.** In the painting, Adam is surrounded by the cloddy earth from which he has been fashioned, while God is *omnipotent* – 'all powerful' – zooming through the heavens surrounded by a swirly crowd of angels!

2 **We are children of God.** The bearded presentation of God and the youthful presentation of Adam indicate the difference in generations. It has also been suggested that the red cloth depicts the womb of God, as it were, and the green ribbon is a symbol of the umbilical cord which nurtures babies in the womb. Here it hangs loose as Adam comes to life – is born.

3 **God is the giver of life.** Note how, in the picture, God stretches out his finger to endow a semi-sleepy Adam with the spark of life. Michelangelo is here depicting *the sanctity of life* – it is sacred and belongs to God.

4 **We are made in the image of God.** In the Bible, God is represented in many ways, including fire, spirit, earthquake and storm. So, although Michelangelo knows that God is beyond our descriptions, here he deliberately paints Adam and God as similar physical beings. Note that the major features, such as the eyes, chest, waist, knees, feet and fingertips, are all carefully aligned. By doing this he emphasises that in a profound sense we are made in the *Imago Dei* – 'the image of God'.

5 **We image God in a mysterious way.** In order to avoid a simplistic physical understanding of how we image God, note that Michelangelo has enclosed God in a 'brain-shaped' cloud which indicates that God is endowing us with intelligence. In so doing, he may be suggesting that these are the faculties by which humanity is able to imitate God through wisdom, knowledge, creativity and love.

6 **Creation is beautiful.** The Bible teaches that God's creation is *good* and *beautiful.* Not only does the well-defined physique of the idealised Adam echo this, but Michelangelo is also painting a reflection of the inner beauty and divinity of the human soul.

Discussion

Having seen how Michelangelo's painting might be understood, are there any aspects of it which might be misleading? If he were alive now, how might he do it differently if the Pope ordered a repaint of the Sistine ceiling today?

Part 2 How its meaning and significance contrast with one other Christian artistic expression of creation

Michelangelo is not the only artist to have tried to express biblical beliefs about creation through art. The contemplation of creation has led to wonderfully imaginative forms of expression whether in film adaptations of the Bible (e.g. *Noah*, 2014), music (e.g. Aaron Copland's *Fanfare for the Common Man*) or poetry (e.g. 'I thank thee God for this most amazing day' by E.E. Cummings.

Elizabeth Wang, meanwhile, is a modern English artist who has depicted many of the Christian mysteries with insight, colour and imagination. You may want to contrast her painting *From the Heart of God* with that of Michelangelo. What features of Catholic belief can you identify here? She writes:

Heart of God by Elizabeth Wang

'From the heart of God has sprung all that exists. Creation is sustained in being by God's power and love. In the very "heart" of God are held and cherished all who live in His love and who have not utterly and eternally rejected him.'

11

Imagine Michelangelo having to climb to the top of the scaffolding every day for four years... Maybe that helped him remember how to depict God and human beings...

C is for...   omnipotent **C**reator and for our status as God's **C**hildren (us).

L is for...   **L**ifegiver (God) and be**L**oved (us).

I is for...   is for **I**mago Dei – God has created us in his **I**mage.

M is for...   Michelangelo's **M**ystery – how does the painting suggest we i**M**age God through using the wisdom of our **M**ind?

B is for...   **B**eauty, which Michelangelo uses to reflect the divine inner life of the soul.

Sample Questions

Identification (AO1): 'What does omnipotent mean?' (1)

Connection/comparison (AO1): 'Compare the imagery of God as Creator in two different artistic forms of expression.' (4)

Evaluation (AO2): 'Michelangelo's painting of *The Creation of Adam* perfectly expresses the Catholic understanding of humanity.' Evaluate this statement. In your answer you should:

- give developed arguments to support this statement
- give developed arguments to support a different point of view
- refer to Catholic teaching
- reach a justified conclusion. (12)

Sistine Chapel, Rome

Differentiation

You might want to research on your own how aspects of the Renaissance movement influenced the religious art of Michelangelo.

Illustrations

The Sistine Chapel at the Vatican in Rome has long been recognised as an amazing masterpiece of religious art. The chapel is filled with various scenes from the Bible, which present the Christian faith as a series of frescoes – paintings done straight onto walls. It includes the story of creation, continues through the stories of the ancient prophets and scenes from the life of Jesus before ending with the Last Judgement. You can take a virtual tour of the chapel here: **http://www.vatican.va/various/cappelle/index_sistina_en.htm**

Unit 1B(i)
Creation Understood through Beliefs and Teachings [AQA Spec.B 3.1.1.2]

CORE IDEA

In this lesson we explore the nature of God understood as creator, as transcendent and as omnipotent in Genesis 1 and 2, and the significance of these beliefs for Catholics.

Part 1 What does Genesis 1 say about God?

In the beginning when God created the heavens and the earth, the earth was a formless void and darkness covered the face of the deep, while the Spirit of God swept over the face of the waters. Then God said, 'Let there be light'; and there was light.

These are the first words of the Bible and they were famously quoted by astronauts on Apollo 8 as they saw the lunar sunrise and for the first time transmitted 'a God's eye view' of Earth.

Words of Wonder: Crazily, although these are the very first words of scripture, they are among the most misunderstood because they are read as scientific history rather than prayerful poetry. We noted above in the very first lesson that the Bible is a library with lots of different types of writing. Genesis 1 is actually an *ancient meditation on the wonder of creation*. How do we know this? Well, we can see that the writing is set out in a sequence of 'days' which are like the different verses of a poem. The days are not literal, but they help to profile how various aspects of creation – the heavens or skies, the land, the seas, vegetation, stars, sun, moon, fish, birds, creatures and human beings – ultimately depend on God for their existence.

God is the *Creator*. Creation is called forth by God's ***Word***. For Christians, creation is not a cosmic accident, nor has it always been there.

a) **God is *omnipotent*** – 'all powerful'. God's Word is the most powerful thing in the universe – more sure and true than any reality we can think of.

b) **God is *transcendent*** – God is 'beyond all things', bringing creation into being but not confined by it. God *surpasses* all our imaginings.

c) **God is *benevolent*** – the universe is '**God-loved**'.

KEY TERMS

Genesis 'Beginnings' = The 1st Book of the Bible.

God as Transcendent = 'Unrestricted' God is beyond our reality.

God as Benevolent = Creation is God-loved.

Part 2   What does Genesis 2 say about God?

Words of Wisdom: In the second chapter of Genesis we find a second ancient meditation which has been even more crazily misunderstood than the cosmic creation. Similar themes of humanity being made in the image of God and the role of the creator are present, but this wisdom poem is more personal and intimate because it is where we first meet Adam and Eve. But beware!

1   This meditation has little twists and is written more like a parable – a story with a symbolic meaning whereby God seems to *limit aspects of his power* and seems *more involved* with us in the human drama.

2   We would be foolish to think the story is about them – it is about *human nature*, **it is about *us!*** You can find one of the best visual depictions of this story in the film *Noah* (2014).

The focus in this lesson is on God, so, comparing the passages from Genesis 1 and 2:

a) Is God the Creator? Genesis 2, verse 4b begins with the familiar idea that God has created heaven and earth – this passage confirms the religious notion that God is the *Creator*.

b) Is God omnipotent? Obviously, as he created the heaven and earth, the answer to this is 'yes', but God seems to *limit his power* – for example, he needs help with the garden (2:5) – so that there is a role for humanity to play in the creation.

c) Is God transcendent? Again, a good question, because instead of creating by word as in Genesis 1, God 'gets his hands dirty' *fashioning* an 'Adam' – a little groundling – from the soil. God's involvement in the world is sometimes called divine *immanence*, but this in no way compromises God's *transcendence* – the view that God's nature *surpasses* all our categories of understanding and is not confined by the physical cosmos.

d) Is God benevolent? Yes – in an intimate way, God seems concerned to make sure his little groundling is provided for and *not alone*. The animals are created and eventually 'Adam' is completed by 'Eve' so that the two become one in love.

Part 3   What do these terms mean for Catholics?

Taken together, the significance of these insights is that Catholics believe everything that exists ultimately belongs to God as *Creator*, and because God is *omnipotent*, *transcendent* and *benevolent*, nothing that happens, no matter how tragic, can ever overpower God's ultimate providence and care. The universe is ultimately a sacred place, suffused with the grace of God, in whom 'we live and move and have our being'.

Explanation (AO1): What does 'transcendence' mean? (1)

Comparison (AO1): Compare how this is understood slightly differently in Genesis 1 and Genesis 2. (4)

 ## Differentiation & Discussion

1 **Are Science and Religion really opposed? Genesis 1 and the Big Bang!** Though some Christian groups teach that the words of this meditation are a literal description of creation completed in seven days, such a view obviously clashes with the commonly held view that the universe began with a huge cosmic explosion billions of years ago. The Catholic Church does not believe there is a contradiction here. In fact, the theory that creation came about from a huge cosmic explosion was first proposed by Georges Lemaître, a Catholic priest (1894–1966). Official Catholic teaching affirms *that* God has created the universe, not how. Indeed, Catholic interpretation has always laid more emphasis on the symbolic understanding of Genesis 1 than on the literal, so some of the arguments that rage about this text can be regarded as misguided. It is as mistaken to analyse Genesis 1 as a scientific document as it would be to think that King Richard the Lionheart of England actually had the heart of a scary cat!

2 **Hoyle vs. Lemaître:** The British astronomer Sir Fred Hoyle (1915–2001) insultingly called Lemaître's idea 'the Big Bang Theory', saying it was about as credible as a whirlwind blowing through an aircraft hangar full of parts and assembling a jumbo jet. Hoyle was not keen that the Big Bang Theory supported the idea depicted in Genesis of a Creator God igniting the universe with light, and the name stuck! Hoyle himself preferred the idea from Ancient Greek thinkers that the universe has always existed and was in 'a steady state' which included 'mini-bangs' that led to the expansion observable in parts of the cosmos.

Memory Moment

God's Cot! To remember these technical terms, it might be helpful to think of the whole of the cosmos cradled like a baby's COT in the kindness or *benevolence* of God:

Creator

Omnipotent

Transcendent

CORE IDEA

In this lesson we explore the belief that we are made in the image of God – 'Imago Dei' – from the texts of Genesis 1 and 2 and how this influences Catholic views on free will, stewardship, the dignity of human beings and the sanctity of life.

Genesis 1 and 2 – a closer look at ourselves!

In Genesis 1 we see:

a) *Imago Dei* and the Sanctity of Life: In the last lesson we looked at God, and now we take a closer look at ourselves. Genesis 1:27 says: 'So God created humankind in God's image, *male and female* he created them.' The text is not to be understood in a *simplistic* sense – indeed, it implies that God is beyond gender and beyond our understanding. However, it does point to *the sanctity of human life* since somehow *together* we image God's likeness in the world.

b) Human Dignity and Freedom: Made in the image of God, we have a special *dignity* and are encouraged to be free, to be fruitful and multiply (Genesis 1:28). In this way, we *share in the creative power of God to re-image* ourselves through our children.

c) Stewardship and Creation: Although the Bible uses 'dominion' or 'subdue' rather than 'stewardship', Catholics understand that just as the plants are entrusted to us for food (Genesis 1:29), God is entrusting humanity with a special responsibility to care for the creation which he has declared to be *good*.

In Genesis 2 we see:

a) *Imago Dei* and the Sanctity of Life: God creates *Adam* from the *adamah* (Genesis 2:7). This is a lovely play on words which can be translated as God fashioning *a groundling from the earth*. It emphasises that Adam is a cloddy body, a human made of humus. **BUT** God then breathes into its nostrils and this little groundling receives its living principle, its **soul.** This represents the *sanctity of life,* which ultimately belongs to God alone. Like the spark in Michelangelo's painting, this inspired parable implies that there is something earthly about us but also something divine (2:7). The completion of humanity as both *male and female* is also key to the text (Genesis 1:23–24).

b) Human Dignity and Freedom: The parable continues with God bestowing **freedom,** a special **dignity,** on the divine groundling, which is granted **a choice** to obey or disobey the command relating to the Tree of Life and the Tree of Knowledge in the middle of the garden (2:17). It is also emphasised that as God becomes more involved and is concerned that 'it is not good for Adam to be alone', so he makes all sorts of animals to see if any are a suitable companion (2:18).

KEY TERMS

Imago Dei = Latin for 'the image of God'.

Free will = Humans can decide their own actions.

Stewardship = Humans caring for the creation.

Dignity = Humans are worthy of respect.

Sanctity of life = Human life belongs to God.

Adam and Eve, fresco on an ancient house, Ardez (Engadine, Switzerland)

You are meant to smile as *Adam* names porcupines and giraffes and ducks but remains glum as a plum, as none of them are an *ezer kenegdo* – a 'helper just like him' (2:20). Again, note that Adam is **free** to 'give names' and he has a surpassing **dignity** – *respectful* of creatures but at liberty to exercise *authority* or *dominion* over them. Humans are *unique*.

c) Stewardship and Creation: As noted above, Genesis 2:5 portrays a poetic scene that the earth is barren since there was no rain and 'no human to till the earth'. In a symbolic way, the text depicts us as partners with God in the care of creation and says that our first call is to be gardeners! Note too that the story continues as God plants Eden, a place of watered wonder, with **every kind** of tree and fruit, which captures the idea of the **goodness of creation** and **God's benevolent** providence (2:8–9).

Memory Moment

In Genesis 1 & 2, God is understood as Creator, as transcendent and as omnipotent. Made in the image of God, humanity is to have a special dignity: free, responsible and respectful of the sanctity of life. The table below gives examples from the scriptures that illustrate these things. Can you find any more?

LEARNING ABOUT	Genesis 1 (1:1–2:4)	Genesis 2 (2:4b–25)
GOD		
Creator	1:1	2:4b
Omnipotent	1:3	2:9
Transcendent	1:4	2:7
Benevolent	1:28	2:18
CREATION		
Full of variety	1:12	2:9
Full of life	1:20	2:19
Good	1:31	2:9
HUMANITY		
Image of God – 'Imago Dei'	1:26	2:7
Male and Female	1:27	2:22
Be fruitful – co-creation	1:28	2:24
Dignity	1:28	2:25
Free	1:28	2:16
Stewards	1:28	2:20
Sanctity of life	1:26–27, 29	2:7

Differentiation

Comparing Two Meditations.	Seven Phases of Creation (Genesis 1)	Seven Aspects of Humanity (Genesis 2)
Genesis 1 identifies seven phases of Creation; can you identify seven phases that unfold in the understanding of humanity?	Light Skies/heavens Land, seas & vegetation Stars, sun and moon Fish and birds Creatures and human beings Chill-out time	Made from e_____ with b_____ of life Gardener – carer for creation Not good to be a_____ Kinship with a_____s One becomes _____ Our first words are a l_____ song. Two become one

 **Sample Questions**

Identification (AO1): What does stewardship mean? (1)

Connection/comparison (AO1): Compare how humans are made in the *image of God* in Genesis 1 and Genesis 2. (4)

Evaluation (AO2): Genesis 1 and 2 together express a rich understanding of God, humanity and creation. Evaluate this statement. In your answer you should:

- give developed arguments to support this statement
- give developed arguments to support a different point of view
- refer to Catholic teaching
- reach a justified conclusion. (12)

 Discussion

In Genesis 2, the parable has God do a mysterious thing. He makes the little groundling fall into a deep death-like sleep and 'takes out a rib and enclosed it in flesh' (2:21). Symbolically this divides the original cloddy humanoid into two sections or sexes. It is then love at first sight when God brings the 'new' groundlet' to the reawakened Adam, who is so delighted that he breaks into Hebrew rap: This at last is flesh from my flesh, bone from my bone. She shall be called woman for she was taken from man (2:23).

OK, so maybe the rap isn't brilliant and you could maybe do better for your valentine – but it is very significant that the first words exchanged in the Bible are a love song (Yo!). So… does this mean that the writer is explaining that it is the desire for relationship which makes us communicate, because on our own, we are incomplete (see Genesis 2:24)? Notice – when we sulk or are frightened we say nothing, but when we are with friends we can't stop talking. We can sometimes be cruel to our friends by NOT talking to them. Is it possible then to imagine a world without words? Does this connect with the way God creates in Genesis 1? What else can words do?

Creation Understood through Sources and Authority [AQA Spec.B 3.1.1.3]

CORE IDEA

This lesson explores the origins, the structure and some key literary forms of the Bible, which Catholics understand to be an inspired library which reveals the Word of God.

Bible – a closer look!

The Bible came about in three distinct phases – oral, written and collected – or *said, read and sorted!*

○ **Oral**. For thousands of years, human communication was *only* through songs and spoken words passed on from generation to generation.

○ **Written**. Israel's meditations, prayers, stories, miracles, battles, triumphs and tragedies emerged like a family history with YAHWEH as their God, and only gradually were written down from around 1000 BC onwards.

○ **Collected**. For centuries, these holy writings were all on separate *scrolls* until better production of parchment allowed pages to be bound together into a *codex* or *book*. Eventually, the *canon* – the 'order' of the collection – was defined by Pope Damasus in AD 382, and today's Catholic Bible is organised as follows:

THE CANON OF THE CATHOLIC BIBLE

HEBREW SCRIPTURES THE OLD TESTAMENT		CHRISTIAN SCRIPTURES THE NEW TESTAMENT	

THE PENTATEUCH	WISDOM BOOKS	GOSPELS	NON-PAULINE LETTERS
GENESIS	JOB	MATTHEW	HEBREWS
EXODUS	PSALMS	MARK	JAMES
LEVITICUS	PROVERBS	LUKE	1 PETER
NUMBERS	ECCLESIASTES	JOHN	2 PETER
DEUTERONOMY	SONG OF SOLOMON		1 JOHN
	WISDOM	**HISTORICAL**	2 JOHN
HISTORICAL BOOKS	SIRACH	ACTS OF THE APOSTLES	3 JOHN
			JUDE
JOSHUA JUDITH	**THE PROPHETS**	**LETTERS OF PAUL**	
JUDGES ESTHER			**APOCALYPTIC**
RUTH 1 MACCABEES	ISAIAH JONAH	ROMANS 2 TIMOTHY	
1 SAMUEL 2 MACCABEES	JEREMIAH MICAH	1 CORINTHIANS TITUS	REVELATION
2 SAMUEL	LAMENTATIONS NAHUM	2 CORINTHIANS PHILEMON	
1 KINGS	BARUCH HABAKKUK	GALATIANS	
2 KINGS	EZEKIEL ZEPHANIAH	EPHESIANS	
1 CHRONICLES	DANIEL HAGGAI	PHILIPPIANS	
2 CHRONICLES	HOSEA ZECHARIAH	COLOSSIANS	
EZRA	JOEL MALACHI	1 THESSALONIANS	
NEHEMIAH	AMOS	2 THESSALONIANS	
TOBIT	OBADIAH	1 TIMOTHY	

Two Testaments

Clearly, then, the Bible isn't one book – it is a *collection* of books, a little library which is full of different kinds of writings. This variety means there is endless possibility for confusion and we need help to make sense of it all. The first way this has been done is to divide the collection into two testaments – two *covenants*.

The first is called the 'Old Testament', which begins with creation and thereafter the various books have as their focus the relationship between God and the children of Israel, who were a 'chosen people'.

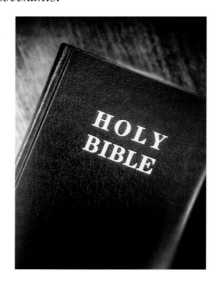

The second is the 'New Testament', and this collection has as its focus the new relationship between humanity and God brought about by Jesus in the Gospels and how his followers, the Church, understood this new revelation in their activities and their letters to each other.

Literary Forms

Law, History, Prophecy and Wisdom are among the more important literary forms in the Old Testament.

1 **Law:** These texts offer guidance for life (the *halakah* – 'way to walk') and are especially exemplified by the famous 'Ten Commandments'. Since this literary form is especially prominent in the first five books of the Bible (Genesis, Exodus, Leviticus, Numbers and Deuteronomy), they are collectively known as 'the Law' or 'Torah'.

2 **History:** The historical books of the Bible tell the story of the chosen people from the time of Joshua, who leads them into the Promised Land in around 1200 BC, through the time of kings such as David and Solomon, until defeats at the hands of Assyria in 721 BC and Babylon in 587 BC led them into exile. Hearing these stories offered *guidance by example* – to imitate heroes such as Gideon and avoid being unfaithful, unjust and cruel like Ahab and Jezebel.

3 **Prophecy:** Less concerned with the *future* than some think, the role of the prophets was primarily to speak God's word to the *present*. They continually challenged the rulers and all the chosen people to remember their covenant love for God in the *past*, and to act justly *in the present* so as to reap God's blessing *in the future*. One of the themes among the prophets was a vision of Israel's future as *the light of the nations*, which included the rule of a *Messiah* whose dominion would have no end (Daniel 7:14).

4 **Wisdom:** These books are sometimes called 'the Writings' and include a variety of prayers and sayings (the Psalms and Proverbs), love poetry and life reflections (Song of Songs and Ecclesiastes), as well as the famous parable of heroic suffering (the story of Job). If prophecy is characterised as *God speaking to the people*, these writings can be understood to be *Israel's response to God*.

20

KEY TERMS

Scripture = The inspired collection of writings called the Bible.

Old Testament = Writings on God and humanity understood through the people of Israel.

New Testament = Writings on God and humanity understood through Jesus and the apostles.

Literary forms = Types of writing such as law, history and prophecy.

many forms can cause confusion on how to interpret the Bible.

Memory Moment

The Old Testament has four divisions in the Catholic tradition: Torah, Historical Books, Wisdom and Prophets. Can you find five books from each in this wordsearch?

R	I	O	L	A	M	E	N	T	A	T	I	O	N	S	E	G	D	U	J
E	U	H	X	W	V	U	T	S	S	R	A	Q	P	O	N	M	L	D	O
H	N	T	C	K	D	P	J	I	H	G	G	F	E	D	A	E	C	B
T	O	P	H	A	M	A	S	S	E	H	G	I	P	J	K	U	A	B	L
S	M	F	H	J	L	E	N	A	A	G	A	E	D	Q	T	H	L	P	C
E	O	M	J	O	N	A	F	I	L	B	H	C	L	E	A	S	G	S	H
P	L	F	C	E	S	C	M	A	E	M	G	T	R	H	I	O	C	G	K
Z	O	O	G	L	X	E	B	H	I	L	S	O	O	J	Q	J	L	E	T
K	S	U	E	P	H	O	A	W	X	G	N	P	E	D	E	H	H	S	O
M	F	P	K	E	J	N	D	S	P	O	B	R	A	H	W	A	A	E	Z
F	O	I	N	F	S	O	W	U	M	J	E	O	L	K	N	B	I	T	S
S	G	Z	V	U	M	I	C	Y	S	M	B	V	G	O	Y	A	D	S	E
U	N	E	X	O	M	E	G	V	I	R	U	E	J	P	K	K	A	A	L
C	O	P	N	I	F	E	Z	A	P	E	E	R	X	I	C	K	B	I	C
I	S	H	U	A	Z	M	H	R	E	T	O	B	W	L	G	U	O	S	I
T	J	A	T	E	P	A	T	M	A	L	H	S	M	E	X	K	A	E	N
I	Q	N	K	I	C	R	S	C	V	Q	O	G	P	U	B	J	D	L	O
V	V	I	C	I	Y	N	A	H	U	M	W	X	O	M	N	W	K	C	R
E	E	A	M	Q	H	A	I	R	A	H	C	E	Z	A	P	H	G	C	H
L	Y	H	Z	G	K	K	I	N	G	S	X	O	D	S	T	O	L	E	C

Torah/Pentateuch
_____
_____
_____
_____
_____

Historical Books
_____
_____
_____
_____
_____

Wisdom
_____
_____
_____
_____
_____

Prophets
_____
_____
_____
_____
_____

 ## Differentiation & Discussion

We take for granted all the forms of communication we have and the ways we can keep records. What are some of the issues regarding traditions passed on by word of mouth? Why were there so few scrolls/books in the ancient world? How did they make sure they were accurate? Hebrew was written without vowels – like TXT MSGS – what problems could arise from that?

The prophets transformed the world with words – just like God in Genesis 1, their words bring light to darkness. Can you think of any examples of someone in our own day who has changed the world by their inspired words?

 ## Sample Questions

Identification Task (AO1): Which of the following is not a literary form in the Bible? Law / Prophets / Historical / Scientific. (1)

Comparison Task (AO1): Explain contrasting ways in which historical writings and those of the prophets are to be understood. (4)

CORE IDEA

Staying with creation themes, we aim to understand how for Catholics the Bible is inspired and is therefore the Word of God, but that it is also a human document with very different literary forms exemplified by Genesis 1 and 2.

Biblical inspiration and the word of God in Genesis 1 & 2

1 **Heaven sent, earth meant:** Now it is vital to remember that Catholics do not believe that this collection we call the Bible was discovered already written like the Book of Mormon, nor was it dictated by an angel, as Muslims believe of the Qur'an. Quite the opposite. The Bible was written by many authors over many years, but the key thing is that the collection *as a whole* is understood by the Church to be *inspired*, or 'God breathed', by the Holy Spirit (see 2 Timothy 3:16).

2 **Word of God:** Catholics believe that through the work of the Holy Spirit, the Bible communicates *God's* wisdom in *our* words and as such can be rightly called 'the Word of God'. It is not just about the past – in reading or hearing the Bible message, God's Word creates, challenges and changes us today. The Bible is a privileged way by which 'the invisible God, out of the abundance of His love, speaks to [us] as friends' (*Dei Verbum* 2).

3 **Genesis 1 and 2** are a good example of how Catholic reading of scripture works.

° One danger that arises from putting very different scrolls together into what looks like *one book* is that people often make the mistake of reading *different* scrolls/books in *the same* way. No! Prayers aren't the same as computer code, love poems aren't law books, parables aren't the same as prophecies, and the passages of Genesis we have studied are also a classic case in point.

° So, Genesis 1:1–2:4 is best understood as an Ancient Meditation on Creation: unlike fundamentalist Christian groups, Catholics do not believe Creation should be understood in a literal sense of seven days, and nor is it to be understood as an early version of the Big Bang Theory.

° Likewise, Genesis 2:4–25 is more like an Ancient Parable or 'Aetiology' – an ancient form of writing which sought to illuminate 'why things are as they are' in story form. Hence it is not *really* about a pretty garden somewhere in the Middle East with a couple of special trees in it, and still less is it to be passed on as a religious contradiction of Darwin's theory of evolution. Rather, it explores the relationship between God, creation and humanity in a vivid, witty parable of our beginnings.

Learned theologians and scientists have always understood this, but simplistic readings of Genesis 1 and 2 lead to unnecessary confusion. It is as if someone were to take a bite out of an apple and be disappointed it didn't taste like a pear. Why should it? It isn't one!

To read one type of text with a different type of mindset is the sort of misunderstanding philosophers call a 'category mistake'. Listen to St Augustine talking about Genesis:

'Now, it is a disgraceful and dangerous thing for an unbeliever to hear a Christian, presumably giving the meaning of Holy Scripture, talking nonsense on these topics and… the writers of our Scripture are criticized and rejected as unlearned men. If they find a Christian mistaken in a field which they themselves know well and hear him maintaining his foolish opinions about our books, how are they going to believe those books in matters concerning the resurrection of the dead, the hope of eternal life, and the kingdom of heaven?'

Literal Meaning of Genesis 19

Summary

The important thing to remember is that through reading Genesis 1 and 2 we are being invited to ponder the relationship between God, humanity and creation. **Properly understood, these are not literal tales about Adam, Eve and a cosmic past, they are about you, me and a cosmic future.** They are about ultimate reality – and the proposition is that we are not outside the drama of life, we are in the midst of it.

Memory Moment

Identify these words or complete these sentences:

1. The Bible is d_____ and _____ and sometimes called the
   W_____ of _____?

2. What 'i' word means 'God breathed'? _____

3. Aetiology is a type of storytelling which reflects on 'wtaata', or
   W_____ t_____ a_____ a_____ t_____ a_____.

4. Catholics disagree with fundamentalists on the s_____
   d_____s of what? _____

5. Genesis 1 and 2 are not s_____, they are religious reflections on
   G_____, h_____y and c_____n.

Q   Sample Questions

Identification Task (AO1): Inspiration means
God-breathed / God-weaved / God-believed / God-deceived? (1)

Comparison Task (AO1): Explain how Catholics understand the Bible as human and divine. (4)

Lost in Translation: Hebrew was originally written without vowels, like TXT MSGS today. You may have made the odd miscommunication because of this, so how might that have affected the passing on of words in the Bible? Why can Catholics be a bit chilled about this?

Image of God: Genesis 1 – humanity is part of the cosmic order and created with a word in the *Imago Dei* – the 'image of God'. In Genesis 2 the writer depicts human beings as *earthly* but receiving the *divine* breath of life. Which account do you prefer, and why?

Old is in the New Revealed: This understanding of inspiration guides how Catholics interpret the scriptures because they believe that the stories and prophecies of the Old Testament foreshadow or *symbolise* the message of the Gospel of Jesus in a special way. This is summed up in a famous phrase regarding the two covenants: *The new is in the old concealed, the old is in the new revealed.*

CORE IDEA

Since creation is good, Catholics believe that there is such a thing as Natural Law which safeguards the sanctity of life and that there is no disagreement between truths of faith, truths of reason and truths of creation.

Tradition & Natural Law

We have seen how the Bible offers insights into God, creation and humanity, but Catholic thinking needs always to recall the 'three-legged' stool, which also includes *Tradition* and *Magisterium*.

One of the insights from Catholic Tradition which it shares with ancient philosophy is that humanity can *learn from creation* that, in a sense, *nature is our first teacher*. Sacred Tradition calls this 'Natural Law' and it forms part of Catholic wisdom for living. It is summed up as follows by the famous saint, Thomas Aquinas (1225–1274):

All activity of reason and will springs from us as being what we are by nature. All reasoning draws on sources we recognise naturally… hence the original guide for our activity should be through natural law.

Summa Theologiae §I-II Q91 a2

Aquinas goes on to identify five things that seem self-evident from 'Natural Law' (**Summa Theologiae §I-II Q94 a2**):

- **Preservation of life, reproduction** and **the nurturing of offspring** appear common to *all creatures*.

- **Orderly living in society** and **pursuit of truth regarding God** are special to humanity because they are part of our *rational* nature.

These 'primary precepts' form part of Catholic tradition. The preservation of life is seen as absolutely fundamental to our nature, hence over the centuries Catholics have always been involved in healthcare and have always been anxious to defend the *sanctity of life* as well as the integrity of human reproduction. Likewise, the Church has always been concerned to influence the way society is conducted and the way it is involved in education to counter ignorance and encourage the pursuit of knowledge.

KEY TERMS

Natural Law = Rules for living which are observable from nature.

Tradition = The *inspired* wisdom captured in the words, customs and lives of Christians.

Magisterium = The *inspired* teaching role entrusted to the Church.

MAGISTERIUM: Creation, Nature, Reason and Faith

1 **Faith and Reason in Harmony.** To complete the 'three-legged stool' when considering Catholic teaching on Creation, it is important to consider how the teaching of the Church harmonises biblical insights, tradition and modern science. The official *Magisterial* teaching of the Church on faith and science can be found in *Gaudium et Spes* ('Joy and Hope'), an important document on the Church in the modern world issued at the Second Vatican Council in 1965. This teaching is very influential and governs the way Catholic scholars approach issues of science and faith. It explains why the Vatican regularly convenes scientific conferences and why science is a core subject in Catholic schools the world over. In exploring the wonder of creation, science has a sacred aspect.

Faith and Reason in Harmony: 'Indeed whoever labours to penetrate the secrets of reality with a humble and steady mind, even though he is unaware of the fact, is nevertheless being led by the hand of God, who holds all things in existence, and gives them their identity. Consequently, we cannot but deplore certain habits of mind, which are sometimes found too among Christians, which do not sufficiently attend to the rightful independence of science and which, from the arguments and controversies they spark, lead many minds to conclude that faith and science are mutually opposed.'

Gaudium et Spes 36

2 **Science versus Church – Fact or Fiction?** Strangely, popular culture often presumes the Church is opposed to science. This is largely based on the 400-year-old case of Galileo, an astronomer from the seventeenth century who had a dispute with scholars who were advising the Pope. Ironically, Galileo was in fact doing experiments to prove the theories of a Polish priest, Nicolaus Copernicus, who had suggested, correctly, that night and day were best explained by the idea that the earth was in an orbit around the sun rather than vice versa. Although Galileo was silenced for a time, scholars continued to wrestle with what were then 'new' theories, and eventually the views of Fr Copernicus and Galileo became mainstream.

Meanwhile, despite what the TV and newspapers might imply, the Vatican has maintained a long-standing and prestigious interest in cosmology. Indeed, the way we date our calendars goes back to 1582, when Pope Gregory corrected an error in the ancient way of marking time in such a way that 13 days 'disappeared' from the diaries of Europe! The Vatican Observatory was founded in 1862 and in Fr Angelo Secchi, it had arguably the most important figure in the development of modern astrophysics. Since that time, light pollution at night in Rome has meant that the Vatican Observatory is now in Arizona, but it is still led by a Jesuit scientist, Brother Guy Consolmagno.

Memory Moment

A two-pronged attack!

Natural Law – Primary Precepts	Magisterium & Science
Preservation of Life	**P**riests involved in Cosmology and Science
Reproduction	**R**eason and Faith must be in harmony
Orderly living	**O**bservatory at Vatican now in Arizona
Nurturing	i**N**dependence of science is rightful
God question	*G*audium et Spes 36

 ## Sample Questions

Identification (AO1): Give two precepts of Natural Law. (2)

Evaluation (AO2): 'The Bible is about the meaning not the making of Creation.' Evaluate this statement giving arguments to support this statement and arguments from a different point of view. You must refer to Catholic teaching and reach a justified conclusion. (12)

 ## Differentiation & Discussion

It is sometimes said that the thinking behind Genesis 2 cannot be reconciled with Darwin's theory of evolution. However, why do Charles Darwin and the Pope agree that they can be reconciled?

'There is grandeur in this view of life, with its several powers having been originally breathed by the Creator into a few forms or into one; and... while this planet has gone cycling on according to the forced law of gravity, from so simple a beginning, endless forms most beautiful have been and are being evolved.'

Darwin, *Origin of Species* (1872), p. 490

'Human beings, even if we postulate a process of evolution, also possess a uniqueness which cannot be fully explained by the evolution of other open systems. Each of us has his or her own personal identity and is capable of entering into dialogue with others and with God himself (#81)... [for] Nature cannot be regarded as something separate from ourselves or as a mere setting in which we live. We are part of nature, included in it and thus in constant interaction with it (#139).'

Pope Francis, *Laudato Si'* (2015)

Copernicus, Secchi and Lemaître were all great priest-cosmologists. But who was Fr Gregor Mendel, and why would he have interested Charles Darwin?

Unit 1D
Creation in Catholic Faith and Practice [AQA Spec.B 3.1.1.4]

CORE IDEA

In this lesson we will learn how care for the environment is another way to 'love our neighbour', how 'stewardship' is a Catholic duty and how belief in the goodness of creation guides CAFOD in its work on sustainability among the poor.

Part 1

1 Narrative: Care for the environment is another way to 'love our neighbour'

The Israelites of Jesus' time were very familiar with the Old Testament teaching to 'love your neighbour as yourself' (Leviticus 19:18), and in the New Testament, Jesus' parable of the Good Samaritan (Luke 10:25–37) is the most famous way in which Jesus taught that 'my neighbour' includes *everyone*. By caring for the environment, Christians do precisely that and help to ensure that the earth and its resources are protected, especially for the world's poor, who are the most affected by problems such as climate change even though they have done least to cause it. In doing this, Christians also act in a neighbourly way towards the environment itself which, just like the traveller helped by the Good Samaritan, is wounded and in need of help.

2 The meaning of stewardship

We have seen how stewardship is a feature of the creation stories in the Bible – we have an especial place in God's creation – one of dominion and co-responsibility. It is also a principle found in the *Tradition* of the Church, particularly Catholic social teaching, and it is also expressed by the *Magisterium* in the way Pope Francis taught that we should treat the environment 'in the sense of responsible stewardship' (*Laudato Si'*, 116).

3 How Catholics might carry out their duty to be stewards

There are many ways that Catholics might carry out their duty to be stewards of creation.

Locally:

° Saving energy by insulating homes and turning off lights.

° Using sustainable energy sources like solar or wind power.

° Cycling or using public transport instead of cars.

° Living simply, reusing and recycling instead of buying new.

° Praising God for the gift of creation and saying grace before meals.

° Avoiding using items like plastic bags that take decades to biodegrade.

KEY TERMS

CAFOD (The Catholic Agency for Overseas Development) =
An International Catholic organisation dedicated to helping the poor.

Sustainability = Help which makes people independent and is not wasteful of resources.

- Eating less meat.
- Getting involved in local schemes like litter picking or community allotments.

Nationally:

- Lobbying (trying to persuade) local MPs or the Prime Minister to ask for more sustainable energy within the UK.
- Marching in peaceful protest against damaging initiatives.

Globally:

- Through organisations such as CAFOD, Catholics campaign for the UK government and world leaders to make policy decisions that protect the earth, cut carbon emissions, promote sustainable energy and help the poorest communities adapt to the impacts of climate change.
- Pray for and fundraise or donate money to support CAFOD's work with vulnerable communities.

Practical Challenge

There are many ways in which we can 'love our neighbour' by caring for the environment that we all share.

Can you add anything to these lists? What are you doing already to be a steward? What more could you do?

Part 2 Narrative: the meaning and significance of CAFOD's work on sustainability as an expression of Catholic beliefs about the goodness of creation

Sustainability: Because Catholics believe that creation is good (Genesis 1:31), they also believe that it should be protected and conserved. Therefore the earth's resources should not be destroyed or used up but should be used in a sustainable way, both for the sake of the earth itself and for the sake of human beings. This means that earth's resources will still be there for future generations to use.

In paragraph 92 and 93 of *Laudato Si'*, Pope francis says that, for Catholics, protecting vulnerable people is always part of protecting the environment. He also says that peace, justice and preservation of creation cannot be separated – every attempt to preserve ecology must also take account of the rights of the poorest and most vulnerable people.

Case study

In the Ugandan village of Nakambi, CAFOD partners have trained Margaret and Lucia to build ingenious wood-saving stoves. These stoves produce less smoke, so are much healthier when cooking indoors, but they also use far less wood, so fewer trees are cut down and the environment is conserved. The old cooking method needed 15 logs to cook one meal; with the new stove, only one log is needed. Margaret and Lucia have now made stoves for every family in their village.

www.cafod.org.uk

They also now sell stoves at the local market to make an income and are training others to make them. This exemplifies what Pope Francis has taught about the environment:

'Efforts to promote a sustainable use of natural resources are not a waste of money, but rather an investment capable of providing other economic benefits…'

Pope Francis, *Laudato Si'*, 191

As well as giving practical help to communities threatened by climate change, CAFOD organises campaigns on climate change, because it believes it is the single biggest obstacle to reducing poverty in our world. Climate change is undoing years of poor communities' work to improve their lives. Destruction caused by typhoons and floods or unpredictable seasons leading to failed harvests leave millions hungry, especially young children who cannot fend for themselves. So CAFOD asks Catholics to lobby UK politicians and world leaders to help prevent climate change pushing people deeper into poverty and to support the transition from using polluting fossil fuels to utilising sustainable energy for all. Find out more at **www.cafod.org.uk**

Practical Challenge

On your own or in groups, try and think of a simple, ingenious item or idea that saves energy or protects the environment in some other way.

Climate Change effects

Memory Moment

This work is NECESSARY!

Neighbour means ...

Everyone so we ...

Care for the ...

Environment as ...

Stewards finding ...

Sustainable ...

Approaches to conserve ...

Resources to give hope to the ...

Young in the poorest countries.

 Sample Questions

Identification (AO1): Which of the following charities work for the global poor? RSPCA / Help the Aged / Pax Christi / CAFOD. (1)

Explanation (AO1): Explain how climate change has had very bad effects in developing countries. (4)

 Differentiation & Discussion

Whether through art, through the Bible, or through Catholic beliefs, tradition and teaching, we are taught to understand ourselves as part of God's creation with a special role in caring for it. How does the teaching on the Sabbath help us to come to terms with this?

Some people have suggested that we have forgotten our intimate connection with Creation so much that there should be a set of commandments devised to remind us not to sin against it. What do you think would be in the top 10?

Incarnation Understood through Symbols [AQA Spec B, 3.1.2.1]

CORE IDEA

By the end of this section you will:

i. Know the meaning and significance of some ancient symbols which represented the beliefs of early Christians about Jesus.

ii. Understand how a belief in the incarnation has influenced Catholic attitudes to religious art and imagery.

iii. Be able to evaluate different Christian views about artistic representations of Jesus in sculptures, statues and art.

Part 1   The meaning of incarnational symbols

Catholics believe that Jesus is God the Son who became a human being in first-century Palestine. This belief is called the incarnation, which comes from the Latin word 'carnis', which means flesh. So Catholic Christians believe that Jesus is God in the flesh. In this chapter we will be looking at three symbols which all represent this belief that Jesus is God incarnate.

The earliest-known depiction of the crucifixion, on the wooden doors of the Basilica of Santa Sabina, Rome. It was carved sometime between AD 420 and 430, about four hundred years after Christ's death. Photo/ Fr Lawrence Lew OP

The most widely recognised Christian symbol today is the cross or crucifix. However, the early Christians never used this symbol. Some scholars think this is because the memory of Jesus' crucifixion was still too fresh in their memories or because crucifixion was still a very real sign of the Roman persecution they continued to suffer. It is also worth remembering that many of the first Christians were deeply rooted in Jewish tradition and they had always resisted the use of images in their worship. Look at the beginning of the Ten Commandments in Exodus 20. Why might this have influenced early Christian attitudes to making images of Jesus?

KEY TERMS

Symbol = Literally 'put together' – a sign with a connected meaning.

Incarnation = God becoming human in Jesus.

Monogram = A symbol made up of letters.

Christogram = A set of letters signifying Christ.

Icthus = The famous 'fish' symbol for Jesus.

Rebus = A coded symbol.

Chi-Rho & Alpha/Omega = Greek monograms for Jesus.

Iconoclasm = The smashing up of religious art or statues.

You shall have no other gods before me. You shall not make for yourself a graven image or any likeness of anything that is in heaven above, or that is in the earth beneath, or that is in the water under the earth; you shall not bow down to them or serve them; for I the Lord your God am a jealous God.

Exodus 20:3–5

Therefore, many of the early Christian symbols were not images at all, but sacred *monograms*. Monograms are symbols made up of letters or initials. And when these monograms are used to refer to Christ, they are called *Christograms*. All of the early Christian symbols used letters from the Greek alphabet because this was the language shared by most of the different cultures and language groups in the many different parts of the Roman Empire at the time of the early Christians.

Icthus

The ICTHUS symbol (in Greek letters it would be written ΙΧΘΥΣ) is a special kind of monogram since the initial letters also make up another word – the Greek word for fish. A word which is made from the initial letters of other words is called an acronym. The Greek letters in the word ICTHUS stand for Jesus (I), Christ (C), God's (TH), Son (U), Saviour (S). Legend has it that early Christians also used this as a *rebus* – a secret code or word puzzle that allowed Christians to identify each other secretly so as to avoid Roman persecution. One Christian would approach another and draw a curve in the sand with her foot. If the person she met drew the other

(handwritten note:) connect to what people went through in the past (persecution)

(handwritten note:) old greek letters people may not understand however could easily be learnt

ΙΗΣΟΥΣ (Ieous) = **Jesus**

ΧΡΙΟΤΟΣ (Christos) = **Christ**

ΘΕΟΣ (Theos) = **God**

ΥΙΟΣ (Huios) = **Son**

ΣΩΤΗΡ (Soter) = **Saviour**

Jesus Christ, God's Son, Saviour

curve to finish the picture of the fish, she would know that the other person was a Christian also. The Icthus Christogram stands for the belief that Jesus is God's Son and Saviour. At the time of Jesus, the term 'son of God' had different meanings. For one thing, it was a title which was often used to speak about the people of Israel in general such as when God describes Israel as his firstborn son (see Exodus 4:22–23) or refer to the prophets specifically. Sometimes, the term 'son of God' does seem to be used to refer to Jesus (see, for example, Matthew 2:15). However, it is also clear that by the time the Gospels were written, the title 'Son of God' had come to have a very special meaning when used to refer to Jesus and that there was some sense in which Jesus was a Son of God like no other:

But Jesus answered them, 'My Father is working still, and I am working.' This was why the Jews sought all the more to kill him, because he not only broke the Sabbath but also called God his Father, making himself equal with God.

John 5:17

An early piece of Christian graffiti from Ephesus which shows the Icthus represented as a circle of overlaid letters. Can you identify each of the Greek letters within the circle?

The title 'Son of God' had become an incarnational title – a way of expressing the belief that Jesus was God himself in the flesh. So the Icthus symbol became a way for the early Christians to mark themselves out as different – as the ones who believed that Jesus is God's Son and Saviour (Icthus).

Many Christians today still use this symbol to mark themselves out as different from their surrounding culture. For example, many Christians put an Icthus symbol on their car to identify themselves as Christians.

Chi-Rho

Another early Christian symbol took the first two letters of the word Christ in Greek (ΧΡΙΣΤΟΣ) and combined them into another Christogram called the Chi-Rho (the name of those first two letters in Greek). This symbol is still common in Catholic churches today and is often featured on baptismal candles, priestly vestments and sacred vessels. The letter which looks like an X is actually the first letter of the word 'Christ' in Greek (equivalent to English 'ch' as it is pronounced in 'loch'). And the letter which looks like a P is actually the second letter of the word 'Christ' in Greek (equivalent to the English 'R').

Photo / Fr Lawrence Lew OP

The Chi-Rho Christogram expresses the belief that Jesus is the Christ since it is made up of the first two letters of the name Christ in Greek. The term 'Christ' means 'anointed one' and is a Greek form of the Hebrew word we translate as 'Messiah'. The Old Testament prophets had predicted the coming of a Christ – a special anointed one of God who would save the people of Israel. For the Jews before the time of Jesus this Messiah was not expected to be God incarnate. So in some senses the Chi-Rho is not an incarnational symbol but a symbol of Jesus' Messiahship. However, over time it became a specifically incarnational symbol as Christianity developed. For example, in the Lindisfarne Gospels and other Gospels produced as illustrated manuscripts around the same time (c. AD 700), the 'Chi-Rho page' was a heavily illustrated page used to mark the parts of the Gospel which describe Christ's birth – the moment the incarnation becomes a visible reality.

The Chi-Rho symbol is evident in many places in Catholic churches – often as part of iron work in the church railings, or on the tabernacle or baptismal font, and frequently on the front of the priest's chasuble. This is also the reason why Christmas is sometimes shortened to Xmas – the X is actually the Greek letter 'Chi', and means 'Christ'.

Alpha and Omega

One of the sets of initials used as a symbol of Christ comes from the scriptures. The book of Revelation uses the symbolism of the Greek letters Alpha and Omega several times. Alpha and Omega (A and Ω) are the first and last letters of the Greek alphabet, and the phrase was common at the time of Jesus as a way to express the sense of something being complete (we still use this in English when we talk of knowing things from A to Z). In the book of Revelation God speaks of himself as the 'Alpha and Omega', and from the very earliest times Christians understood the title to refer to Jesus also. The Alpha and the Omega are clearly incarnational symbols since they refer to God first and foremost, and if we also apply the title to Jesus we are clearly saying that the man Jesus was God incarnate and that the Son of God was there at the beginning of all things (he is the Alpha) and that he will be there at the end of all things (he is the Omega). It is another way of speaking about Jesus as sharing the eternity of God. The Alpha and Omega are still used today to refer to Christ in the Catholic liturgy of the Easter Vigil as the priest inscribes a cross, the year and the Alpha and the Omega letters into the wax of the Paschal candle. The Paschal candle is the symbol of the risen Jesus.

Paschal candle

1. Christ yesterday and today

(*the priest cuts a vertical line*);

2. the Beginning and the End

(*he cuts a horizontal line*);

3. the Alpha

(*he cuts the letter Alpha above the vertical line*);

4. and the Omega

(*he cuts the letter Omega below the vertical line*).

5. All time belongs to him

(*he cuts the first numeral of the current year in the upper-left corner of the cross*);

6. and all the ages

(*he cuts the second numeral of the current year in the upper-right corner of the cross*).

7. To him be glory and power

(*he cuts the third numeral of the current year in the lower-left corner of the cross*)

8. through every age and for ever. Amen

(*he cuts the fourth numeral of the current year in the lower-right corner of the cross*).

Part 2 The incarnation and Catholic attitudes to religious art and imagery

At different points in the history of Christianity there have been disputes about whether it was right to make and display images of God, Jesus and the saints in churches. For the most part, Christians have been happy to make religious images and to use them as an aid to worship. However, there are two periods of Christian history where there has been strong opposition to the use of images. During these periods those who disagreed with images have objected to them so strongly that they have destroyed religious art and statues.

Iconoclasm — *protestants breaking away from the Catholic Church bc of indulgence of images + statues wanted a simpler church*

The first of these periods was in the eighth and ninth centuries, when members of a movement in the Eastern Christian Church called 'iconoclasm' destroyed images and persecuted those who still used images in their worship. Iconoclasm comes from two Greek words which, combined, mean 'breaker of images'. In the image on the right, from the Church of Hagia Irene in Istanbul, the mosaic of Christ which would usually have filled the half-dome of the ceiling has been replaced by a simple cross. This is believed to be an example of iconoclastic art from this period.

Hagia Eirene, Saint Irene Church, Istanbul/ Turkey

Photo / © Jeff Veitch

The second period when images were destroyed was during the Protestant Reformation of the sixteenth and seventeenth centuries. Many of the Reformers showed their rejection of Catholicism by destroying Catholic art and images, which they saw as an insult to God. Many cathedrals in the UK and across Europe contain evidence of this later period of iconoclasm.

The image above is from Durham Cathedral. It shows a block of stone where all of the figures, one of whom is Jesus, have been defaced.

Catholic attitudes to religious art and imagery

Catholics have always rejected iconoclasm and have always been comfortable using representational art in their churches and homes as a focus for worship. This Catholic attitude has been influenced by the belief in the incarnation. Catholics believe that because the invisible God made himself visible in Jesus Christ, it is appropriate to represent Jesus in human art forms. Because God has made himself visible in Jesus, Christians can make Jesus visible in religious art as a focus for worship and an aid to prayer.

Part 3   Statues and sculptures of Jesus

In almost all Catholic churches there will be at least one statue of Jesus. For example, most Catholic churches will have a crucifix displayed in a prominent place. What is the meaning and significance of representations of Jesus like this for Catholics?

The crucifix

A crucifix is a cross which has on it a figure of Jesus. This figure is usually the figure of the crucified Jesus – wounded and dying. It can also, however, be a figure of the risen Christ – risen and glorified with the cross behind.

For Catholics, the crucifix is a reminder of the importance and significance of Jesus' death and resurrection. The death and resurrection of Jesus is the event which Catholics believe saves them and opens the kingdom of heaven for them. In crucifixes which show a wounded Jesus, there will usually be a nail through each of Jesus' hands and a single nail which pierces both of his feet. There will also be a wound in the side of Christ, which is a reference to the end of John's Gospel (John 19:34) where Jesus' side is pierced rather than his legs being broken. From his side flowed blood and water, which is often interpreted as a sign of the two sacraments of Baptism and the Eucharist. This is a symbol that the Church begins with the death of Jesus. The wounds in his hands, feet and side are sometimes referred to as the five wounds of Christ.

In many Catholic churches there will be a large crucifix at the front of the church which Catholics might well use as a focus for their prayer – an image to look at and speak to which reminds them of the person to whom they pray. This reminds Catholics of the reality of the incarnation – that Jesus became a real human being who lived and died. The physical reality of the crucifix reminds Catholics of the physical reality of the historical incarnation.

Different Christian views about artistic representations of Jesus

In Catholic churches these representational figures of Jesus will be venerated and used in worship – either in the liturgy or as the focus for private prayer. For example, in most Catholic churches there will be places where worshippers can light candles in front of sacred statues or images and make individual prayers and petitions before these statues or images. As well as these statues of Jesus, there may well be many other examples of devotional art – statues of Our Lady and the saints, icons and religious images, frescoes or paintings of scenes from the scriptures and so on.

In most Protestant Christian churches there will be little, if any, Christian art. Most Protestant churches are characterised by the absence of any forms of representational art and by buildings which are elegant but simple in their design and decoration. There will be no statues and there are unlikely to be any religious images. Even where there are examples of art work or images, these would never be the subject of veneration and would never feature as part of the worshipping life of the community.

What are the reasons for these differences, and what are the arguments for and against the uses of images of Jesus as an aid to prayer?

Arguments **FOR** the use of statues/images	Arguments **AGAINST** the use of statues/images
Images and statues of Jesus are useful reminders of the person who is the focus of worship, just as photographs of loved ones are reminders of the loved ones. Catholics would argue that they are not worshipping the statue but the one whom the statue signifies.	Many Christians believe that the use of statues and images in worship is against the second commandment (Exodus 20:3–5), which forbids the worship of idols. Some Christians think that any images of Jesus are idols since human art can never capture the mystery of God.
Catholics would reply that the commandment against idols cannot be a reference to the use of statues since the author of Exodus also relates the command to the making of statues and figures in, for example, the decoration of the ark (Exodus 25:18–20).	Other Christians might well reply that the problem is not the making of statues or images for decorative purposes but the use of these images as a focus for prayer and devotion – this is what turns the objects into idols.
Catholics would further argue that the acceptance of the veneration of images of Jesus is a way of remaining faithful to the belief that God became a real human being who was visible and tangible, just like the images.	Other Christians might reply that God became incarnate as a human being, not as stone or wood, and so the only way to honour the reality of the incarnation is to serve the presence of Jesus in other people.

Study of one statue that represents the incarnation

This is a statue by Malcolm Brocklesby at Mount Grace Priory in Osmotherley, in northern England. Malcolm was born in Sheffield and led a very full life as a top scholar, elite rower, professional rugby player, mining engineer, rural activist, family man and sculptor. This intriguing piece is called 'The Madonna of the Cross'.

Now, to be clear, this has nothing to do with a famous American singer! 'Madonna' is an ancient Italian title for Mary, the Mother of Jesus.

What religious insights do you see in this statue?

From the front it depicts Mary. Who is she holding? What is in her gesture? Is it defiance? Offering? How has the artist connected life and death in this picture? How do you think it looks from the back? Is it just like a simple cross – or a crucifix? In what ways does it connect with incarnation? Can you find Bible references that link with this sculpture?

If you are interested, you might want to compare this statue with *The Pietà* by Michelangelo and spot similarities and differences.

Alan Murray-Rust/ Geograph Project Collection

Doctrine Detectives

[handwritten: → Church coming together (Bishops popes). ← where they meet]

The Second Council of Nicaea in AD 787 condemned the iconoclasm which had become a growing movement in the early Church:

[handwritten left margin: Sorting out use of images replying to inoclasm.]

'… we declare that … the production of representational art … is quite in harmony with the history of the spread of the Gospel, as it provides confirmation that the becoming man of the Word of God was real and not just imaginary, and as it brings us a similar benefit. For, things that mutually illustrate one another undoubtedly possess one another's message.

[handwritten right margin: not a problem art is doing no harm.]

[handwritten right margin: Statues could remind you of your belief in God & religion]

Given this state of affairs and stepping out as though on the royal highway, following as we are the God-spoken teaching of our holy fathers and the tradition of the Catholic Church – for we recognise that this tradition comes from the Holy Spirit who dwells in her – we decree with full precision and care that, like the figure of the honoured and life-giving cross, the revered and holy images, whether painted or made of mosaic or of other suitable material, are to be exposed in the holy churches of God, on sacred instruments and vestments, on walls and panels, in houses and by public ways, these are the images of our Lord, God and saviour, Jesus Christ, and of our Lady without blemish, the holy God-bearer, and of the revered angels and of any of the saintly holy men.

The more frequently they are seen in representational art, the more are those who see them drawn to remember and long for those who serve as models, and to pay these images the tribute of salutation and respectful veneration. Certainly this is not the full adoration in accordance with our faith, which is properly paid only to the divine nature, but it resembles that given to the figure of the honoured

[handwritten right margin: remind them of faith /morals to pray worship.]

and life-giving cross, and also to the holy books of the Gospels and to other sacred cult objects. Further, people are drawn to honour these images with the offering of incense and lights, as was piously established by ancient custom. Indeed, the honour paid to an image traverses it, reaching the model, and he who venerates the image, venerates the person represented in that image.'

How do the fathers of the Second Council of Nicaea defend the use of art and imagery as a focus for worship?

Memory Moment

THE GREEK ALPHABET

Which of the Greek letters are used in the monograms and Christograms described above?

Minuscule Form	Unical Form	Greek Name	English Pronunciation	English Name
α	A	άλφα	a - father	Alpha
β	B	βητα	b - bat	Beta
γ	Γ	γαμμα	g - gave	Gamma
δ	Δ	δελτα	d - dog	Delta
ε	E	έψιλον	e - met	Epsilon
ζ	Z	ζητα	z,dz - adze	Zeta
η	H	ήτα	e - they	Eta
θ	Θ	θητα	th - thin	Theta
ι	I	ίωτα	i - machine	Iota
κ	K	καππα	k - king	Kappa
λ	Λ	λαμδα	l - lake	Lambda
μ	M	μυ	m - man	Mu
ν	N	νυ	n - noon	Nu
ξ	Ξ	ξι	x, ks - axe	Xi
ο	O	όμικρον	o - log	Omicron
π	Π	πι	p - pea	Pi
ρ	P	ρω	r, hro - more	Rho
σ,ς	Σ	σίγμα	s - sing	Sigma
τ	T	ταυ	t - to	Tau
υ	Υ	ύψιλον	u - toon	Upsilon
φ	Φ	φι	ph - phone	Phi
χ	X	χι	kh, ch - Bach	Chi
ψ	Ψ	ψι	ps - lips	Psi
ω	Ω	ώμεγα	o - tone	Omega

 Sample Questions

Identification (AO1): Which of the following is not a Christian symbol? The fish / the dove / the crucifix / the crescent moon? (1)

Explanation (AO1): Explain two ways in which beliefs about the incarnation have influenced Catholic views about statues. (4)

Evaluation (AO2): 'Ancient Christian symbols have little value for believers today.' Evaluate this statement. In your answer you should give arguments to support this statement as well as arguments to support a different point of view. You should refer to Christian teaching and reach a justified conclusion. (12)

He did become human remind us not just some tail.

should we have a picture of Jesus could worship statue rather than its representation.

Could help people focus to pray.

Incarnation Understood through Beliefs and Teachings [AQA Spec B, 3.1.2.2]

CORE IDEA

By the end of this section you will:

i. Know the meaning of the word 'incarnation'.

ii. Understand how this belief is expressed in those passages of Scripture which refer to Jesus as Incarnate Son and Divine Word.

iii. Be able to evaluate the extent to which the titles 'Son of Man' and 'Son of God' as found in the Scriptures express the Catholic belief in the incarnation of Jesus as fully God and fully man.

Part 1   Incarnate Son and Divine Word

The Gospel writers expressed their belief in Jesus as the Incarnate God in different ways in their Gospels. Mark does not have a meditation on the birth of Jesus, but the Gospels of Matthew, Luke and John have important insights which all emphasise that Jesus can be uniquely understood as the Son of God, being born not of mere human desire, but of divine love.

Matthew and Joseph

° Matthew's version seems to be written from the point of view of Joseph. Joseph finds out his fiancée is with child. He is not best pleased. Oh no – what is going to happen? Women could be stoned for being unfaithful in such a way. Well, panic not. The name 'Joseph' calls to mind the 'dreamer' from the Old Testament, and this Joseph is also told *in a dream* by an *angel* that Mary is with child through the power of God and so he takes her as his wife (1:24).

> In Matthew, Jesus is called 'Immanuel', 'God is with us' (1:23). 'Im' means 'with'; 'anu' means 'us'; 'el' means 'God'.

Luke and Mary

○ Luke's account seems to be written from the point of view of Mary, who has an encounter *with an angel* who tells her she is to bear God's child by the Holy Spirit. She is somewhat discombobulated (1:29) – let's not forget the custom of betrothal meant she was probably a young woman of maybe 15 or 16 at the time. She also knew this was a dangerous thing for her – people talk! So she immediately goes to visit her cousin Elizabeth far away in the hills who is also unexpectedly expecting!

The Annunciation, fresco by Joseph Erns Tunner (1830) in church Chiesa della Trinita dei Monti. Renata Sedmakova / Shutterstock.com

John and the Cosmos

- John's account of the incarnation is more than the story of a new life – he smashes the categories of space and time and suggests that we are talking about a new Creation! Why? In the Jewish tradition, God had created all things by *his word* – e.g. in Genesis God says: 'Let light be, and light is!' (1:3).

- Now think about it ... this means that the connection between Creation, Us and God is *God's Word*. In the same way that scientists today talk about the Higgs boson particle, in Greek and Hebrew thinking there was the theory of a connecting cosmic principle which they called 'The Logos', from which we get the word 'logic', but which usually means *Word*. John knows this and he is proposing that the connecting *logic* of all things is found in Jesus – the *logos* made *flesh*. Just as the first *divine word* created cosmic light for us *to see* by, so the same *divine word* made flesh (1:14) is light for humanity *to live* by.

- John is saying: 'Listen'. God's word has created the Cosmos and now God's word can be heard, seen, touched *in a human life!* Jesus is God's love word spoken in flesh – the *divine word* is spoken, the unseen God has been finally revealed by the One who is nearest to the Father's heart (1:18).

Part 2   Son of Man and Son of God

Son of Man

The title 'the Son of Man' is the title most commonly used by Jesus in the Gospels to refer to himself – it occurs more than one hundred times.

It has fascinated scholars down the centuries because it has three intriguingly different meanings:

a) Lowly

Sometimes it was used to indicate the lowliness of human beings compared with God's greatness. For example, Psalm 8:4 – 'What is man that you are mindful of him, a *son of man* that you care for him?' Is Jesus implying: 'I'm an ordinary guy – just like you'? For example, see Matthew 8:20 – foxes have their holes and birds their nests but the Son of Man has no place to lie down.

b) Prophetic

The title is used in the Book of Ezekiel 93 times. 'Son of Man' is the way of God addresses the prophet (e.g. Ezekiel 2:1). Is Jesus implying: 'I am a prophet like Ezekiel, speaking as God commands me?' See, for example, Luke 19:10 – 'the Son of Man came to seek out and to save the lost', just like the prophets of the covenant.

c) Cosmic

In the book of Daniel, the title refers exclusively to a heavenly figure who will come to signal the end of time and the arrival of God's judgement. It is worth reading this passage:

'I saw in the night visions,
and behold, with the clouds of heaven
there came one like a son of man,
and he came to the Ancient of Days
and was presented before him.

And to him was given dominion
and glory and a kingdom,
that all peoples, nations, and languages
should serve him;

his dominion is an everlasting dominion,
which shall not pass away,
and his kingdom one
that shall not be destroyed.'

Daniel 7:13–14

> **KEY TERMS**
>
> **Incarnate Son** = Jesus is God's love enfleshed in a human life.
>
> **Divine Word** = Jesus is God's love spoken in a human life.
>
> **Son of God** = Jesus is divine, Son of the Father.
>
> **Son of Man** = Jesus is human, Son of Mary.
>
> **Messiah** = 'Anointed One' in Hebrew.
>
> **Christ** = This is not Jesus' surname – it means 'Anointed One' in Greek.

Is Jesus implying that he is the cosmic figure who will be given authority over all the earth? See, for example, Luke 18:8 – 'When the Son of Man comes, will he find any faith on earth?'

Conclusion? 'Son of Man' is almost the perfect title for Jesus to choose if he wanted to convey both a human and a divine message. On the one hand, ordinary. On the other, cosmic. In between, prophetic. Altogether – mystery!!

Son of God

The title 'Son of God' has now become a shorthand way for Christians to express their belief that Jesus is the incarnate Son of God.

It is worth noting that 'son of God' was at one level a general term of belonging to God. For example, the kings of Israel, especially David (see Psalm 2:7), are referred to as God's sons. Sometimes the whole nation of Israel itself was referred to as God's son (see Exodus 4:22). In the New Testament, too, other people apart from Jesus are referred to as sons of God. For example, the author of Luke's Gospel refers to Adam as God's son (Luke 3:38).

However, we have seen above how Matthew, Luke and John convey the idea that Jesus was God's only son, having a unique status. Mark's Gospel also begins with a similar assumption: 'The beginning of the good news of Jesus Christ, Son of God' (Mark 1:1) – and spookily, it is the unclean spirits who seem to realise this more quickly than the disciples (3:11).

St Paul, who wrote his letters to Christians probably before even the Gospels were completed, is also as clear as St John in saying that the incarnation reveals Jesus as 'son of the Father' and 'the icon of the invisible God, the first born of all creation' (see Colossians 1:3 and 1:15).

The clearest statement from the disciples comes from Peter, who refers to Jesus as 'the Christ, the Son of the Living God' in Matthew 16:16.

Please note, however, that this did not make Jesus some kind of spooky, floaty, non-human avatar. The whole point was that the Son was divine but 'emptied himself' and took on human nature (see Philippians 2:7 and John 1:14).

This 'fully human, fully divine' truth can be seen among the earliest Christian generations. Ignatius of Antioch writes: 'We have also as a Physician the Lord our God, Jesus the Christ, the only-begotten Son and Word, before time began, but who afterwards became also man, of Mary the virgin' (Ignatius' letter to the Ephesians, chapter 7).

Son of God and Son of Man

Crucially, the Bible brings these two titles together right at the climax of the story of Jesus in his trial before the High Priest. We are used to 'courtroom dramas' on TV, and at this point in Matthew we read: *And the High Priest said to him, 'Are you the Messiah, the Son of God?' Jesus said, 'You have said so. But I tell you hereafter you will see the Son of Man seated at the right hand of Power and coming on the clouds of heaven.'* At this point the High Priest tears his clothes and the whole assembly condemns Jesus to death for the crime of blasphemy in claiming to be Son of God and Son of Man.

Luke 22:67–71 is a very similar account, and John 19:7 has this use of Son of God at the centre of the trial. Note, however, that in Mark's version (14:62) it is perhaps even more blasphemous. Jesus in his answer to the High Priest uses the Holy Name **I AM** (see Exodus 3:14). Use of this name was enough to knock people over (see John 18:6), but by claiming to be Son of Man, Son of the Blessed One and uttering I AM, Jesus has declared himself equal to God in power and glory – and for this he was to die.

Conclusion

Christians have many titles for Jesus, which, as we have seen, include Son of Man, Son of God and Divine Word. However, the central belief is that Jesus is God in the flesh. This is the mystery of the incarnation. Jesus is not an avatar, he is fully God and fully man.

🛡 Bible Detectives

Compare the similarities and differences (below) between Matthew and Luke, and then between John and Genesis.

MATTHEW	LUKE
1. Does an angel announce Jesus' birth?	
Matthew 1:20	Luke 1:26–38
2. Who is the angel talking to in each case?	
Matthew 1:20	Luke 1:26–38
3. Is Jesus' mother a virgin named Mary?	
Matthew 1:18,23	Luke 1:27
4. Is Mary engaged to a man called Joseph?	
Matthew 1:19	Luke 1:27
5. Is the unexpected news worrying as well as wonderful?	
Matthew 1:19	Luke 1:29,39
6. What is the child to be called?	
Matthew 1:20–21	Luke 1:32,35
7. Does Mary conceive by the Holy Spirit?	
Matthew 1:18,25	Luke 1:35
8. Is Jesus born in Bethlehem?	
Matthew 2:1	Luke 2:4
9. Would that be in a house then?	
Matthew 2:11	Luke 2:7
10. Who comes to visit?	
Matthew 2:1–11	Luke 2:8–20
11. Are the Holy Family displaced persons, asylum seekers or economic migrants?	
Matthew 2:13–23	Luke 2:4,39–40
JOHN 1	**GENESIS 1**
12. Do they start the same way?	
John 1:1	Genesis 1:1
13. How does God create?	
John 1:3	Genesis 1:3
14. Does that include everything?	
John 1:3	Genesis 2:1
15. And the first thing is?	
John 1:4	Genesis 1:3
16. How is God imaged?	
John 1:14	Genesis 1:27
17. Has no one seen God?	
John 1:18	Genesis 1:26

Memory Moment

This section of the course requires that you remember the meaning of the titles Incarnate Son, Son of Man, Son of God and Divine Word. Having studied symbols, monograms and Christograms in the last session, can you design some to help you remember key points regarding the Christian understanding of these mysteries?

 Sample Questions

Identification (AO1): Which of the following titles is not used of Jesus? Son of Man / Son of Zebedee / Son of Mary / Son of God (1)

Explanation (AO1): Explain two Christian understandings of the incarnation. Refer to Christian beliefs in your answer. (5)

Evaluation (AO2): 'The notion that Jesus is the Divine Word is irrelevant to believers today.' Evaluate this statement. In your answer you should give developed arguments to support the statement, as well as arguments to support a different point of view. You should refer to Christian teaching and reach a justified conclusion. (12)

Incarnation Understood through Sources [AQA Spec B, 3.1.2.3]

CORE IDEA

By the end of this section you will:

i. Know the key moral teachings presented by Jesus in Matthew 5:1–48 and Matthew 25:31–46.

ii. Understand what is meant by the teaching of Irenaeus that 'the glory of God is a human being, fully alive'.

iii. Be able to compare and contrast how the doctrine of the incarnation is expressed in *Dei Verbum* 4 and in *Verbum Domini* 12.

Part 1 Scripture and the incarnation of Jesus as a source of moral authority

We know that Catholic teaching works with evidence from three sources: Scripture, Tradition and Magisterium. First we look at Scripture. Christians believe that Jesus is God incarnate and so they look to Jesus as a human being who understands perfectly what it means to live as God requires.

The Gospel writers in different ways make this clear.

- Matthew chapter 5 is called 'The Sermon on the Mount' because Jesus 'went up on the mountain … and taught them' (Matthew 5:1–2). This connects what Jesus is doing with Moses and the Ten Commandments, which are more accurately translated as the *Ten Words* that were given by God on Mount Sinai.

- While Mark (7:37) and Luke (9:43) also emphasise that Jesus embodied an astonishing new way to live, St John is probably clearest when he calls Jesus 'the *Word* made Flesh'. By doing so, he also calls to mind the same 'Ten Words' of Moses in the Old Testament (Exodus 20:1–17). John is saying that the way to live in love and in God *has been revealed in a human life.* Jesus who is the ONE WORD shows us how to live the meaning of the TEN! Jesus is *the* example.

- This is because he is both a human being and God. In this way, Jesus becomes a source of moral authority for Christians. That means they try to follow Jesus' example and abide by his teaching as the trustworthy guide to how to live a virtuous life.

Part 2 Jesus as moral teacher

Matthew 5:1–12 The Beatitudes

The Sermon on the Mount opens with a list of 'blessings'. These blessings are called the beatitudes, after the word *beatus*, which is used in Latin translations of the Bible. Beatus means *blessed, happy, fortunate* or *content.*

KEY TERMS

Virtue = A desirable moral quality.

Beatitudes = The Kingdom blessings of Matthew 5.

Heresy = Mistaken belief.

Docetism = Jesus wasn't human.

Adoptionism = Jesus wasn't divine.

Virtue The word 'virtue' is a translation of the Greek word 'arete', which means 'an excellence'. Virtues are the personal qualities demonstrated by a person who lives a morally good life – they are the different types of moral excellence. The virtues are the different ways in which a human being can show moral excellence: e.g. courage, wisdom, justice, self-control, etc. The Gospels as a whole presents Christians with the teaching and example of Jesus as a man who lives out the virtues perfectly.

Blessings or curses? Yet the Beatitudes are a strange list. Jesus lists nine different sorts of people who he declares are happy or fortunate, some of whom don't sound fortunate at all – for example, those who mourn and those who are persecuted. In this passage Jesus is deliberately turning upside down the world's understanding of what it means to be blessed or fortunate. He is making it clear that those who have suffered in this life, especially those who have suffered for the sake of God, are the greatest in the Kingdom.

The Kingdom of God which Jesus talks about seems to be more of a *vocation* than a *location*. You have to *put yourself out to get yourself into* the Kingdom – for example, through meekness, being a peacemaker, acting justly, being honest and pure in heart and being merciful rather than vengeful.

Be-attitudes? For this reason, some preachers refer to them as the *Be-attitudes*. Whatever life throws at us, we have to first *be* confident that God remains close to us because we *are* God's children. In fact God is even closer to those who suffer than he is to those who swan through life, because his Son too was destined to suffer.

Matthew 5:13–48: The fulfilment of the Law

The Law is changed, not ended: In the list of demands Jesus makes, each one begins with the phrase, 'You have heard that it was said … but I say to you', and then Jesus makes a reference to a particular law from the Torah as it is recorded in the Hebrew Bible and in the Christian Old Testament.

The Beatitudes

1. When Jesus saw the crowds, he went up the mountain; and after he sat down, his disciples came to him.
2. Then he began to speak, and taught them, saying:
3. 'Blessed are the poor in spirit, for theirs is the kingdom of heaven.
4. 'Blessed are those who mourn, for they will be comforted.
5. 'Blessed are the meek, for they will inherit the earth.
6. 'Blessed are those who hunger and thirst for righteousness, for they will be filled.
7. 'Blessed are the merciful, for they will receive mercy.
8. 'Blessed are the pure in heart, for they will see God.
9. 'Blessed are the peacemakers, for they will be called children of God.
10. 'Blessed are those who are persecuted for righteousness' sake, for theirs is the kingdom of heaven.
11. 'Blessed are you when people revile you and persecute you and utter all kinds of evil against you falsely on my account.
12. 'Rejoice and be glad, for your reward is great in heaven, for in the same way they persecuted the prophets who were before you.'

The Law is written on hearts, not stones: Jesus goes beyond *obedience* to the Law and challenges his disciples to change their *disposition*. For example, don't just avoid adultery, stop being slimey and avoid lusting after people. You'd be better off without an eye than to be destroyed by desire (5:27–30)! This emphasis of Jesus fulfils the prophecy of Jeremiah 31:33 that the New Israel would have the Law *written on its heart* rather than on tablets of stone.

Don't be complacent: Jesus seems particularly harsh on those who 'talk the talk but don't walk the walk'. He says that *unless your righteousness exceeds that of the scribes and Pharisees, you will never enter the kingdom of heaven* (Matthew 5:20). As far as Jesus is concerned, it is worse for you to become religiously smug, snooty and moralistic than to be a sinner who knows your need of God's mercy.

Matthew 25:31–46: The parable of the sheep and the goats

Later on in his Gospel, Matthew drives home this very point. In this parable, Jesus presents his listeners with a vivid image of the Last Judgement where God will separate the righteous from the unrighteous, like a shepherd separating sheep and goats. The righteous are rewarded for the charity they have shown to their neighbour, and the unrighteous are punished for ignoring those in need. Jesus makes the demand to help those in need even stronger by claiming that he is present in those in need, and helping or ignoring the needy is equivalent to helping or ignoring Jesus:

'Truly, I say to you, as you did it to one of the least of these my brothers or sisters, you did it to me … as you did not do it to one of the least of these, you did not do it to me.' This radical teaching suggests that Jesus is imaged by humanity where we least expect him to be. It's an unusual spin on the mystery of the incarnation since Mother Teresa called this 'seeing Jesus in his most distressing disguise'. It is as if we need to put on special 'kingdom glasses' to recognise Jesus in our brothers and sisters, and this parable yields a clear set of moral commands that can be drawn:

1 Feed those who are hungry.

2 Give drink to those who are thirsty.

El Llaminer 'the sweet' - Pastisseria de Cal Pla. Photo/Janet Fearns

3 Welcome strangers.

4 Give clothes to those who have none.

5 Visit the sick.

6 Visit those in prison.

St Francis with a leper. Photo/Janet Fearns

These six demands are very closely linked to a list of good actions which in the Catholic tradition are called the 'Corporal Works of Mercy'. Find out what they are and show how they are linked to the parable of the sheep and the goats.

Tradition and the incarnation of Jesus as a mirror on humanity

Irenaeus was a Christian writer and thinker from the second century who was Bishop of Lugdunum, which sounds like a place from *Lord of the Rings* but is better known as Lyon in France. In one of his books, *Against Heresies*, he reflects on the meaning of the incarnation for Christians. The following extract is taken from Book 4, Chapter 20, paragraph 7 of *Against Heresies*:

> From the beginning the Son is the one who teaches us about the Father; he is with the Father from the beginning. He was to reveal to the human race visions of prophecy, the diversity of spiritual gifts, his own ways of ministry, the glorification of the Father, all in due order and harmony, at the appointed time and for our instruction: where there is order, there is also harmony; where there is harmony, there is also correct timing; where there is correct timing, there is also advantage.
>
> The Word became the steward of the Father's grace for the advantage of men, for whose benefit he made such wonderful arrangements. He revealed God to men and presented men to God. He safeguarded the invisibility of the Father to prevent man from treating God with contempt and to set before him a constant goal toward which to make progress. On the other hand, he revealed God to men and made him visible in many ways to prevent man from being totally separated from God and so cease to be. The glory of God is a human being, fully alive and what brings life to a man is the vision of God. If the revelation of God through creation gives life to all who live upon the earth, much more does the manifestation of the Father through the Word give life to those who see God.

One of the reasons the incarnation is so important to Irenaeus is that because Jesus is both God and man he can teach human beings who the Father is. This is because, as God, he knows who the Father is, and as a human being, he can teach other human beings about him. The incarnation makes Jesus an intermediary between God and humanity.

Here, too, Jesus stands as the man between two worlds, like a two-way mirror: reflecting man back to God and God down to man. He is the perfect expression of the Glory of God and shows through his life that he brings eternal life to all human beings.

Irenaeus presents the same idea again in this sentence. As God, Jesus is able to show human beings who God is. As man, he is able to offer back to God the gift of all humanity in himself. Jesus becomes like a broadband connection – through him human beings download God, and through him human beings are uploaded to God.

Conclusion

For Irenaeus, the incarnation was a perfect reflection of both God and humanity, with Jesus as the line of symmetry where the two halves of reality – God and human beings – meet.

Magisterium and the incarnation of Jesus

Church Teaching: The incarnation has been a theme for two recent documents of the Church's magisterium: *Dei Verbum*, one of the constitutions of the Second Vatican Council, and *Verbum Domini*, an Apostolic Exhortation of Pope Benedict XVI.

Keep the Balance: Both documents are trying to capture the important truth of the incarnation, that Jesus is both fully God and fully man. To stress either Jesus' humanity or his divinity leads to mistakes, or what the Church calls heresy.

Avoid Heresy! A heresy is a mistaken belief. To stress the divinity of Jesus and neglect his humanity leads to a heresy which sees Jesus' humanity just as a sort of human disguise. This heresy is known as *docetism* (from a Greek word which means 'to seem'). To stress Jesus' humanity and forget that he is also God leads to thinking of Jesus as simply a good man who God just 'adopted' as his Son. This heresy is called *adoptionism*. In the two extracts that follow, both documents together reflect both the full humanity and the full divinity of Jesus.

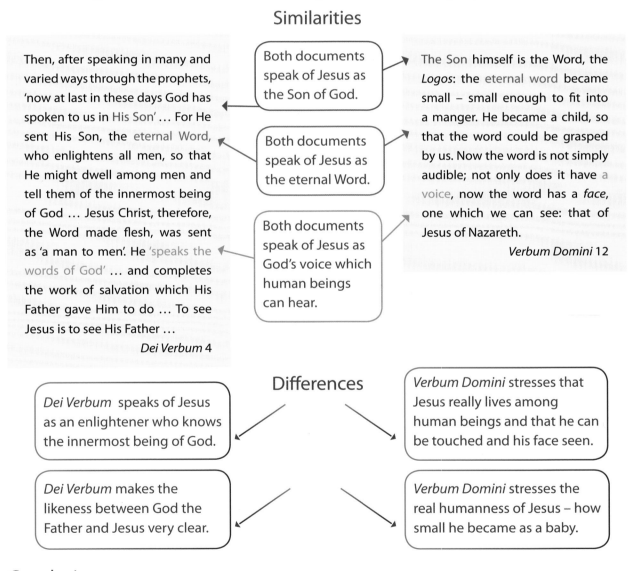

Similarities

Then, after speaking in many and varied ways through the prophets, 'now at last in these days God has spoken to us in His Son' … For He sent His Son, the eternal Word, who enlightens all men, so that He might dwell among men and tell them of the innermost being of God … Jesus Christ, therefore, the Word made flesh, was sent as 'a man to men'. He 'speaks the words of God' … and completes the work of salvation which His Father gave Him to do … To see Jesus is to see His Father …

Dei Verbum 4

- Both documents speak of Jesus as the Son of God.
- Both documents speak of Jesus as the eternal Word.
- Both documents speak of Jesus as God's voice which human beings can hear.

The Son himself is the Word, the *Logos*: the eternal word became small – small enough to fit into a manger. He became a child, so that the word could be grasped by us. Now the word is not simply audible; not only does it have a voice, now the word has a *face*, one which we can see: that of Jesus of Nazareth.

Verbum Domini 12

Differences

- *Dei Verbum* speaks of Jesus as an enlightener who knows the innermost being of God.
- *Dei Verbum* makes the likeness between God the Father and Jesus very clear.

- *Verbum Domini* stresses that Jesus really lives among human beings and that he can be touched and his face seen.
- *Verbum Domini* stresses the real humanness of Jesus – how small he became as a baby.

Conclusion

The truth of the incarnation, that Jesus is fully God and fully human, is seen in all three legs of the stool: Scripture, Tradition and Magisterium. This belief that God made himself visible and tangible to human beings is the key reason why Catholics believe God is still present to us in the sacraments – which is the topic of the next chapter.

Memory Moment

Complete this table to help you picture how Jesus fulfils but does not abolish the Law in the Sermon on the Mount:

	'You have heard that it was said…' **Old law**	'But I say to you…' **Law fulfilled**	Illustration
Murder and Anger	You shall not murder; and whoever **murders** will be liable to judgement. (See Deuteronomy 5:17, 16:18)	Do not be **angry** or insult other people. (See Matthew 5:22–26)	
Adultery and Lust	You shall not commit **adultery**. (See Deuteronomy 5:18)	Do not even look at another person with **lust** in your heart. (See Matthew 5:27–30)	
Divorce	Whoever divorces his wife must give her a certificate of **divorce**. (See Deuteronomy 24:1–4)	**Do not divorce** at all. (See Matthew 5:31–32)	
Swearing Oaths	Do not **swear** falsely, but do what you have sworn. Keep your promises. (See Deuteronomy 23:21)	**Do not swear** at all. (See Matthew 5:33–37)	
Revenge	An eye for an eye and a tooth for a tooth. Make sure your **revenge** is not excessive. (See Deuteronomy 19:21)	**Do not take revenge** at all. (See Matthew 5:38–42)	
Love	**Love your neighbour** and hate your enemy. (See Leviticus 19:18)	**Love everyone** – even your enemies. (See Matthew 5:43–48)	

Q Sample Questions

Identification (AO1): Who said: 'The glory of God is a human being fully alive'? Zeus, Irenaeus, Amadeus, Thaddeus. (1)

Explanation (AO1): Explain how two of the beatitudes can be said to fulfil the Law of Moses. Refer to Christian understanding in your answer. (5)

Evaluation (AO2): 'Jesus has moral authority whether or not he was the Incarnate Son of God.' Evaluate this statement. In your answer you should give developed arguments to support the statement and arguments to support a different point of view. You should refer to Christian teaching and reach a justified conclusion. (12)

Incarnation Understood through Practices [AQA Spec B, 3.1.2.4]

CORE IDEA

By the end of this section you will:

i. Understand what is meant by grace and the sacramental nature of reality and how Catholic beliefs about these are influenced by a belief in the incarnation.

ii. Know the names of the seven sacraments and Catholic beliefs about the effects of these sacraments on each stage of a person's life.

iii. Be able to evaluate Catholic beliefs about abortion and the difference a belief in *imago Dei* makes to these beliefs.

Incarnation, grace and the sacraments

In the last section, Pope Benedict spoke of Jesus as 'the face of God for human beings'. This is one very helpful way of understanding the significance of the incarnation for Christians. There is a famous story of a little girl who is begging her mother to stay with her at bedtime because she is afraid of the dark and doesn't want to be left alone. Her mother tries to comfort her by telling not be afraid because God is always with her. But the little girl says, 'I know God is always with me but sometimes I need God with skin on.'

What the little girl means is that sometimes as human beings we need more than words – we need something we can touch and hold. For many Christians this is a way of understanding why God became a human being. And for Catholics it is why Jesus, the human face of God, leaves the Church with visible (things we can see) and tangible (things we can touch) signs of his presence. These signs Catholics call sacraments.

Meanwhile, we all know that the last words said by friends before parting are often the most significant. At the Last Supper Jesus left his disciples *something to do* in remembrance of him – the ritual meal which has continued as the sacrament of the Eucharist. Moreover, Jesus' last words in the Gospel of Matthew are a promise, through baptism, to be with his Church 'always, until the end of the age' (Matthew 28:19–20). In this way the sacraments are a fulfilment of this promise of his presence, the incarnation extended through time.

The sacraments and grace

- A sacrament was famously defined by St Augustine as a 'visible sign of invisible grace'.

- Grace comes from the Latin word '*gratia*' which, in turn, is a translation of the Greek word '*charis*', and both words mean 'gift'.

- Christians tend to understand grace first through the loving **creation** of human beings, and second through the love of God in Jesus Christ which brings about **salvation** from sin.

- Grace thus begins and ends in love. God loved us into creation and also loves us enough to save us from our daft decisions, wrong-headed actions and stupid attitudes.

KEY TERMS

Grace = The free gift of God's love.

Sacrament = A visible and effective sign of God's invisible grace.

Abortion = The deliberate ending of a life in the womb.

51

- Grace is a word for God's actions in the world and for the power and love of God at work in human beings. Grace cannot be earned or deserved but is always a free gift from God offered to all.

- The sacraments are moments of grace, special moments of God's love and blessing upon the faithful.

The sacramental nature of reality

The first way that God makes his love visible to human beings is through the creation of the world. Catholics believe that at some level the whole of the created world is a sacrament of God's love and presence. This means that the whole of reality is in one sense 'sacramental'.

The second way is more specific. St John says that 'God is Love', and there is a famous song, 'Ubi Caritas', which, translated, says: 'Where there is true love, God is there.' Catholics believe that sacraments are special signs of God's love for human beings – particular moments of God's grace that help believers to be aware of God's presence in their lives.

The incarnation and the sacramental nature of reality

The incarnation is the mystery that makes sense of sacraments. Christians believe that God loved the world so much that he became a human being in Jesus Christ. Because God was happy to enter into the world and live in it, this means that ordinary things in the world can become signs of God's love and presence: water, oil, bread and wine. And it was through these ordinary things, Catholics believe, that Jesus chose to make himself present for all time through the sacraments of the Church.

Sacraments are 'efficacious signs instituted by Christ and entrusted to the Church' *CCC 1131*. Why is the word 'efficacious' used here?

The seven sacraments

Seven Signs: In Catholic tradition there are seven different rituals which celebrate and make real the presence of God to those who believe in him. These are: baptism, reconciliation, communion, confirmation, matrimony, Holy Orders, anointing of the sick.

Effective Signs: The Catechism calls the sacraments 'efficacious', which means that they make things happen – the sacraments are not just signs, they also bring about, or make real, the thing which they are a sign of. So the sacrament of reconciliation is not just a sign of God's forgiveness, it is also the sacrament which brings about the forgiveness of sins; the sacrament of marriage is not just a sign of the love of two people for each other, it is the sacrament which means that a man and woman are now husband and wife.

The Form Matters! The seven sacraments have a central sign or symbolic action (sometimes called the 'matter') and some special words (sometimes called 'the form') which together are the moment when what is signified is made real for the believer.

Christ-begun: Each of the sacraments is believed to have been 'instituted' by Christ. That means that Jesus is the one who first celebrated these sacraments or instructed his disciples to celebrate them.

> ### 🛡 Doctrine Detectives
>
> Each of the seven sacraments is believed to be initiated by Christ. Find a passage in scripture to support this claim for each of the seven sacraments. Here is a list of scripture passages to help you get going. See if you can find others.
>
> Matthew 28:18–20, John 3:5, Acts 8:14–17, Acts 9:17–19, John 6:1–15, John 6:25–71, Mark 14:22–25, Luke 7:47–50, Matthew 16:13–19, James 5:13–16, Mark 10:2–12, Acts 14:22–23
>
> After this investigation, do you think Catholics are justified in claiming that Jesus instituted the seven sacraments?

Memory Moment

Illustrate and complete this chart to help you memorise the essential aspects of the sacraments.

Sacrament	Matter (the symbolic sign or action)	Form (words spoken)	Effect
Baptism (from the Greek word *baptizein*, which means to immerse in water)	Water	Priest: 'I baptise you in the name of the Father, and of the Son and of the Holy Spirit.'	The person is cleansed of sin and becomes a member of Christ's body, the family of God, the Church.
Confirmation (from the Latin word *confirmare*, which means to strengthen)	Oil of chrism	Bishop: 'Be sealed with the gift of the Holy Spirit.'	The person is strengthened by the Holy Spirit to become a missionary witness to the Gospel.
Eucharist (from the Greek word *eukharistia*, which means thanksgiving)	Bread and wine	Priest: The whole of the Eucharistic prayer, including: 'This is my body… this is my blood.'	The body and blood of Christ is received, which brings about the forgiveness of sins, makes the person an ever-closer member of Christ's body and joins them in ever-closer union with God and the other members of the Church.
Marriage (from the Latin word *maritatus*, which means to join together)	The marital consent of the man and woman	Couple to each other: 'I take you for my lawful wedded wife/husband, to have and to hold from this day forward, for better, for worse, for richer, for poorer, in sickness and health, to love and to cherish until death do us part.'	A man and woman become husband and wife.
Holy Orders	The baptised candidate	The prayer of consecration over a deacon, priest or bishop which follows the laying on of hands.	A man becomes a deacon, a priest or a bishop.
Reconciliation (from the Latin word *reconciliare*, which means to bring together again)	Unsurprisingly, 'sins are the matter' – contrite confession is why you're there!	Priest: 'I absolve you from your sins in the name of the Father, and of the Son and of the Holy Spirit.'	A person's sins are forgiven and they are reconciled to God.
Sacrament of the Sick	Oil of the sick	Priest: 'Through this holy anointing may the Lord in his love and mercy help you with the grace of the Holy Spirit… May the Lord who frees you from sin save you and raise you up.'	A person receives forgiveness of their sins and comfort and strength in their illness or advanced years.

continued overleaf

Illustration	Bible passage

Incarnation, *Imago Dei* and abortion

You will remember that Catholics believe that every human being is made *imago Dei*, in the image of God. Because of this belief, Catholics believe every human being has a dignity and a worth which can never be taken away. This in turn means that innocent human beings must never be deliberately harmed or killed. For Catholics this includes unborn children, from the very first moment of conception. Conception is the moment when an egg is fertilised inside a woman at the very beginning of pregnancy. At this stage, the new human being is only one large cell (the correct biological term for it is zygote). This cell doesn't look like a human being. Why do Catholics believe it is a human being?

The incarnation and the unborn

One of the reasons is connected to the account of Jesus' own conception in the Gospel of Luke. Jesus is conceived differently to all other human beings, since he is conceived 'by the Holy Spirit' – without a human father (see Luke 1:26–38). This moment when Jesus begins to exist in the womb of Mary is the moment of the incarnation, so from the very beginning of his human existence, God is present in this single cell, in the human being who at that moment is only one large cell, who will grow to be Jesus of Nazareth. After Mary receives the message from the angel, she goes to visit her cousin Elizabeth, who says to her:

'And how has it happened to me, that the mother of my Lord would come to me? For behold, when the sound of your greeting reached my ears, the baby leapt in my womb for joy.' (Luke 1:43–44)

In this passage, it is clear that Elizabeth's own baby (John the Baptist) has recognised the presence of Jesus in Mary's womb and has leapt for joy at his presence. Both of the unborn children in this passage are real human beings. John is six months old in Elizabeth's womb, and Jesus is days, if not hours, old, in Mary's womb. A belief in the incarnation, and the stories that relate to it, is one of the reasons Catholics believe that a human being begins to exist from the moment of conception. For this reason, Catholics believe that abortion is always wrong, because the deliberate killing of an innocent human being is always wrong.

Arguments for and against abortion

Not everyone agrees with the Catholic belief that abortion is always wrong.
In the table below are some arguments against the Catholic position, and
the responses that Catholics would make.

Catholic arguments against abortion	Criticisms of the Catholic position	Catholic responses to these criticisms
From the moment of conception, a new human being begins to exist and therefore killing it is wrong.	The zygote is only one cell big. It doesn't have any human features and it has no brain. It can't think or feel anything. Killing it is no more significant than cutting off a fingernail.	A human being's worth is not determined by his or her abilities but by the fact that he or she is a human being. Killing a human being who is only one cell big is not like cutting a fingernail since the zygote is a new and unique human life.
The moment of conception is the only obvious place to point to as the beginning of a new person because this is the first time a new and unique life begins to exist. The only change that happens after that is that the cells divide and grow.	The zygote has the potential to split into two (or even three) and become identical twins. If that is true, it can't be the beginning of a person since two persons might come from it.	It is true that the zygote might split and become more than one person, but this new human life will never be less than one person. The zygote is the beginning of at least one new human life – maybe more.
Since a zygote is at least one new human life, deliberately killing it is always a kind of murder.	Calling abortion 'murder' is unhelpful language because many women who have abortions do it only after a lot of thought and often reluctantly. Especially in cases of rape, abortion may be seen as the lesser of two evils.	The Gospel can be summed up as a call to 'protect the weak'. Rape is one of the most serious crimes – but it is wrong to respond to one serious sin (rape) by committing another. Aborting the innocent baby who bears no responsibility for the crime against its mother denies someone their right to life.

 Sample Questions

Identification (AO1): Give two Catholic beliefs about the importance of life that can be found in the Gospel account of the visitation of Mary to Elizabeth. (2)

Explanation (AO1): Explain how two actions of Jesus in the Gospels can be said to have 'instituted' a sacrament. (4)

Evaluation (AO2): 'Sacraments are an extension of the incarnation.' Evaluate this statement. In your answer you should give developed arguments to support the statement, as well as arguments to support a different point of view. You should refer to Christian teaching and reach a justified conclusion. (12)

CORE IDEA

In Unit 3 we explore the Catholic understanding of the glory of God and belief in the mystery of God as Triune (or Trinity). Expressions of this belief in music, Scripture and Tradition are explored, along with the authority and influence of the Magisterium and the practice of prayer.

Unit 3A – Expressions of the Glory of God in Music. In this section we explore the notion of the glory of God through music.

Art: trying to express the inexpressible?

In Unit 1A (AQA Spec. B 3.1.1.1) we noted that various forms of art (e.g. painting, sculpture, film, poetry, music) have tried to express something of the wonder of the Christian notion of creation. There is a long tradition in Catholic Christianity of using various art forms to communicate some of its wisdom, insights and glories.

Love: How many songs can you write down that are to do with the topic of love – a happy experience of love, a sad experience, betrayal, love gone sour, love that lasts a lifetime, and so on? Off the top of my head, here are just seven (they probably reveal a lot about my age!):

'Careless Whisper' (George Michael)

'It Must Have Been Love' (Roxette)

'(Everything I Do) I Do It For You' (Bryan Adams)

'Hero' (Enrique Iglesias)

'Make You Feel My Love' (Bob Dylan/Adele)

'Someone Like You' (Adele)

'We Found Love' (Rihanna)

Adele, Helga Esteb / Shutterstock.com

There are probably hundreds of thousands of songs that we could have listed. And if we add to that number all the books, poems, plays, films, articles, TV and radio programmes, paintings and sculptures that deal with the topic of love, we would be talking about millions of amorous allusions! *When it comes to love, we can never say it all!*

Life: Which songs or pieces of music mean something to you? Why? Do the music and the words remind you of something? Do they take you back to a holiday (literally a 'holy-day') place? Or maybe to an important time in your life? Does the song or music take you somewhere in your imagination? Does it 'evoke' – trigger – a memory or a feeling? *When it comes to life, we can never say it all!*

Divinity: Music and all art are trying to express something which is, ultimately, too rich, too mysterious and too full of meaning ever to be adequately shared. G. K. Chesterton once claimed, 'All art is born when the temporary touches the eternal' – that is, it is an attempt by human beings living in time to express something beyond time. The artist senses that the cosmos is absolutely chock full of mystery and meaning and will always be trying to express the inexpressible. The religious word for 'inexpressible' is *ineffable* because *when it comes to the divine, we can never say it all*.

KEY TERMS

Signs/symbols = Material things (i.e. things we can see, touch, hear, taste or smell) that point to spiritual things.

Glory = The term *doxa* in Greek and *kabod* in Hebrew refers to the inexpressible majesty of God.

Ineffable = Means 'indescribable, unutterable, beyond description'.

Sacred music = Music and song that is written to honour God.

Mass setting = Music which accompanies the *acclamations* of the Mass.

Not the same as:

Hymns = The traditional term for *songs* sung during worship.

Why and how is music used in Mass?

The Glory of God:

In the scriptures *glory* means the utterly inexpressible splendour and majesty of God and the worship, honour and praise that should therefore be given by human beings to God. In Mass the Church tries to use several means to remind us of this great mystery. One such means is **music**.

The Vatican Council teaches that there are many signs and symbols used by the Church in worship, but music and sacred song are among the most important. '"The musical tradition of the universal Church is a treasure of inestimable value, greater even than that of any other art" (*Sacrosanctum Concilium*, 112)' (CCC 1156).

- Why? Music is *evocative* – it acts as a trigger to raise minds and hearts to God. That is why it is used in the Mass and in other forms of prayer and worship.

- Music expresses *joy* – the disciples were accused of being drunk on Pentecost day as they praised God (Acts 2:13), but they were filled with the joy of the Spirit.

- Music expresses *love* – St Augustine used to say, 'He who sings prays twice' (CCC 1156). He said: 'A song is a thing of joy; more profoundly, it is a thing of love. Anyone, therefore, who has learned to love the new life has learned to sing a new song ... so let us love God with the love he has given us' (*Sermon* 34:1).

Types of Music:

- **Psalms:** these biblical hymns and songs have been used in Eucharist and prayer since the beginning of Christian worship and are rooted in the ancient Jewish traditions of the Temple. They express every type of emotion – joy, sorrow, anger and love. All of life is made a prayer, and even in death, psalms like Psalm 23 are a great consolation. There is always a psalm at Mass, and ideally it should always be sung.

- **Plainchant:** sometimes called Gregorian Chant after Pope Gregory the Great, who revised and promoted this form of worship music. Often associated with monasteries and convents, it is has an *ethereal* – 'mysterious' – tone which helps some people to pray in a contemplative way.

- **Traditional Hymns:** These are classic hymns of praise to God which have stood the test of time. Although they may have old-fashioned phrases and are normally best accompanied by the organ, they often express doctrines (such as Trinity), seasons (such as carols at Christmas) or special devotions (such as Eucharist). They originate from all the major Christian traditions and are often sufficiently well known to be used at family occasions such as baptisms, weddings and funerals.

St Gregory the Great by Carlo Saraceni (1579–1620).

- **Contemporary Worship:** Vatican II taught a renewed emphasis within Catholicism on singing by the congregation, which led to Church musicians developing melodies that people could easily sing and words they could easily understand. Taking on modern folk or popular musical forms, songs such as 'Make Me a Channel of Your Peace', 'Do Not Be Afraid' and 'Here I Am Lord', as well as non-Catholic classics such as 'I Could Sing of Your Love Forever', are typical of this type of worship. Although some people think that modern wording and melody lack mystery, for others this type of music is more exciting in terms of rhythm and instruments, more accessible in terms of music, and more emotionally engaging in terms of lyrics.

Mass settings

Sometimes prayers in the Mass are put to music:

- **Kyrie/Lord Have Mercy:** 'Lord have mercy, Christ have mercy, Lord have mercy.' The music helps people acknowledge their failings and seek God's mercy.

- **Gloria/Glory to God:** 'Glory to God in the highest, and on earth peace to people of good will…' is an ancient hymn of praise to the Trinity, just after the *Lord Have Mercy*.

- **Gospel Acclamation/Alleluia:** a joyful acclamation just before the proclamation of the Gospel in order to worship Jesus, who renews his people as the life-giving Word of God.

- **Sanctus/Holy, Holy, Holy:** a chant of praise and worship, based on Isaiah 6:3, showing how the congregation unite their praise of God's glory with that of the angels and saints in Heaven.

- **Memorial Acclamation:** at the heart of the Eucharistic Prayer, the priest says, 'The mystery of faith', and the people reply with an acclamation which celebrates the mystery of redemption – e.g. 'Save us Saviour of the world, for by your cross and resurrection, you have set us free.'

- **Doxology/Great Amen:** 'Through him, with him and in him…' This is the great prayer of praise of the Trinity that closes the Eucharistic Prayer, to which the whole congregation say 'Amen' ('So be it!').

- **Agnus Dei/Lamb of God:** 'Lamb of God, you take away the sins of the world, have mercy on us … grant us peace.' This is sung as the consecrated bread is broken. The faithful are reminded to give glory to Jesus, the lamb who has been broken and sacrificed for the sins of the world.

Memory Moment

G... is for the **G**lory of God... which music points to.

L... is for the **L**iturgy, the Church's public worship, in which music can be used so fruitfully.

O... is for the **O**ffering of praise to the glory of God.

R... is for the sung **R**esponses made by the people – for example, when singing the psalm.

Y... is for the **Y**oung people who are such an important part of the music in many parishes today, and for the kabod **Y**HWH, the glory of God, whose praises they sing.

🛡 Music Detectives: Rock 'n' Roll Glory and Classical Mass

Rock 'n' Roll 'n' Glory

It is not only hymns that are sung in church. The mega-successful U2 originally sang in a prayer group. Their song 'Gloria' is another example of 'ineffable praise' – they left most of the chorus in Latin. Check out '40' by the same group. Bands too numerous to mention have done similar things – e.g. 'Awake my Soul' by Mumford & Sons; 'Shackles' by Mary Mary. A good example of a thanksgiving song is Beyoncé's 'God Made You Beautiful' – but what other examples of glory and thanksgiving to God can you find among contemporary artists?

The Classics

'Gloria' by U2 forms part of a long tradition. Classical artists have long tried to 'say the unsayable' by using music, and if you haven't heard an excerpt from Handel's 'Hallelujah Chorus', then see if you can track it down. If you want to know what the glory of heaven might sound like, then check out *Spem in Alium* by the English composer Thomas Tallis (1505–85). Going back further, can you find anything by the best-selling medieval diva Hildegard of Bingen? Her 'For the Creator' is a plainchant classic!

Mass Settings

Try to listen to some different Mass settings from the internet. The *Missa Luba* is a very striking African setting with an especially evocative *Sanctus* – 'Holy Holy'. From the classical tradition, Mozart's *Requiem* is a famous funeral Mass setting, and for a contemporary contribution, check out the work of CJM.

Ⓠ Sample Questions

Identification (AO1): Which of the following is a Eucharistic acclamation? A psalm / a sermon / a hymn / the mystery of faith. (1)

Identification and Explanation (AO1): Give two arguments as to why some people prefer contemporary songs in worship. (4)

*— interest younger generation
could touch peoples
emotions more help
them feel close to God*

Evaluation (AO2): 'Music is the only way that Christians can truly express the glory of God.' Evaluate this statement, giving arguments to support the statement and arguments from a different point of view. You must refer to Catholic teaching and reach a justified conclusion. (12)

The Trinity Understood through Beliefs and Teachings [AQA Spec. B 3.1.3.2]

CORE IDEA

In this section we explore the Christian teaching that God is a Trinity of persons – the Father, the Son and the Holy Spirit who are mentioned by the Nicene Creed – and we look at some of the roots of this teaching in Scripture and how it sheds light on the first three verses of the Bible – Genesis 1:1–3.

Prepare to be mind-boggled: the mystery of the Trinity

The Trinity 'is the central mystery of Christian faith and life' (CCC 234). The Trinity is sometimes called the Triune God (that is, the 3–1 God!). Along with the Incarnation, it is the most controversial aspect of Christianity, and sharply differentiates it from Judaism and Islam.

The Nicene Creed is the most commonly used creed in Christian Churches, and this statement of belief includes the following:

I believe in one God, the Father almighty…

I believe in one Lord Jesus Christ, the only begotten Son of God…

I believe in the Holy Spirit, the Lord, the giver of life.

One God: In common with Judaism and Islam, Christianity teaches that there is *only one God* ('monotheism'), but that God has gradually revealed Godself in history not just as divine Love, but as Love *Loving* – as Father, Son and Spirit.

Not Three Gods: It is important to remember that, as CCC 253 says, 'The Trinity is One. We do not confess three Gods, but one God in three persons.' 'Trinity' is the shorthand word for this: 'Three Whos (Father Son Spirit), one What (God).'

Wild or Wonderful? Although at first glance this idea might seem crazy, for the Christian, it is the supreme example of a divine *paradox* – an *apparent* contradiction that is *actually* true. An everyday example of

The Trinity by Leandro Bassano (1557–1622). Photo / Didier Descouens

this is 'you have to be cruel to be kind' – hence your teacher *lovingly* prepares *horrible* tests for you. God is revealed as Triune not to offend human rationality but to lead humanity into deeper truth.

KEY TERMS

Trinity/Triune = The teaching of the Church that the nature of God is one and three.

Creed = A statement of belief. The word 'creed' comes from the Latin word *credo*, which means 'I believe'.

Nicene Creed = This creed was first formulated at Nicaea in AD 325 and was completed in AD 381 at the Council of Constantinople, and it is used in Christian Churches to the present day.

Trinity and Reality: Christianity teaches that the whole of creation is held together by God's love (Colossians 1:17). The inner nature of God is *relationship,* just as the inner nature of reality is *relationship*. The Unity of God is described as Love, and the distinctions or persons explain the *loving*. God is not static, God is ultra-*dynamic* – the famous poet Dante describe God as an ever-changing interplay of love *that moves the Sun and other stars.*

The roots of the Trinity in the Scriptures

Though the actual word 'Trinity' is not used in the Bible, Christianity arrived at this conclusion in order to explain all the data about God that is found in the scriptures (Deuteronomy 6:4, Matthew 3:16–17, Galatians 4:6).

God as ONE:

'Listen, Israel: the Lord our God is the one Lord.'

Deuteronomy 6:4

To repeat: Christianity teaches that there is only one God. Jesus himself taught this: 'You must love the Lord your God with all your heart, with all your soul, and with all your mind. This is the greatest and the first commandment' (Matthew 22:37–38).

God as TRIUNE:

'As soon as Jesus was baptised [by John the Baptist in the river Jordan] he came up from the water, and suddenly the heavens opened and he saw the Spirit of God descending like a dove and coming down on him. And a voice spoke from heaven, "This is my Son, the Beloved; my favour rests on him."'

Matthew 3: 16–17

The first Christians realise that while God is one and in Heaven, God also seems to be mysteriously present in a man called Jesus. And they grasp that there seems to be a connection between the Father and the Son called the Spirit of God. God is revealed at the same time in three "instances" or persons.

God as PRESENT:

'The proof that you [Christians] are children [of God] is that God has sent the Spirit of his Son into our hearts: the Spirit that cries, "Abba, Father."'

Galatians 4:6

Once again we read of a triple reference to God (1) who sends the Spirit (3) of his Son (2) which enables human beings to call on God as 'Abba, Father'. Abba is a lovely Aramaic word for how a child would speak – 'Dadddyeee' (though generally only used in teenage years when trying to wangle some more spending money out of the old fella). With the Spirit (3) in their hearts, believers are able to do what Jesus the Son of God (2) does – namely, call God 'Father' (1). It is like becoming an 'adopted' child of God.

Trinity in Genesis?

God/Lord/Spirit: As the early Christians began to articulate this mystery, the shorthand in the New Testament became by and large that 'God' = God the Father; 'Lord' or 'Word' = Jesus the Son; and 'Holy Spirit' = Spirit. This is important for the way that the early community then began to re-read their ancient scriptures, not least the first words of Genesis:

'In the beginning God created the heavens and the earth. Now the earth was a formless void, there was darkness over the deep, and God's spirit hovered over the water. God said, "Let there be light," and there was light.'

Genesis 1:1–3

Understanding God as triune, Christians began to see hints of that mystery in the scriptures.

'In the beginning God created the heavens and the earth.' (v.1)

° God is Creator – creation is not some random accident, nor has it always existed; it comes into being because of the eternal God – Father, Son and Spirit. How?

'God's spirit hovered over the water.' (v.2)

° The Church interprets this verse to be a hint of the Holy Spirit's presence, the third person of the Trinity. 'The Holy Spirit is at work with the Father and the Son from the beginning' (CCC 686). This is the life-giving Spirit, the one professed by the Nicene Creed to be 'the Holy Spirit, the Lord, the giver of life'.

'God said, "Let there be light," and there was light.' (v.3)

° The *Father* speaks. Creation is called into being by a divine *Word* which is *light* – this theme is taken up in John's Gospel (1:1–4) and is summed up by the Nicene Creed: 'I believe in God the Father Almighty, Creator of heaven and earth ... and in the only begotten Son, God from God, light from light, *through whom* all things were made.'

'God said, "Let us make humankind in our own image."' (v.26)

° The Christian understanding of God as Trinity meant that this text could be understood as God creating humanity in a mystery of *relationship*, a mystery of *love* – male–female – whose ONE-ness becomes THREE as their offspring become the image of their love.

Memory Moment

Visuals: As well as classic Father–Son–Spirit depictions, St Patrick famously tried to illustrate the Trinity using a shamrock. Feel free to copy the Father–Son–Spirit 'shamrock' diagram and do some green shading.

Family – Pope St John Paul II sometimes used Genesis 1:26 to introduce the idea of the Trinity as a *communion of persons* united in *one* love.

Friendship – Not everyone is called to family life. Aelred of Rievaulx once said 'God is Friendship', and if you imagine three close friends, they are each unique, but so is their affection *together* – in fact, that affection is what designates them as what they are – friends. Do your own selfie – three whos, one what – Trinity!

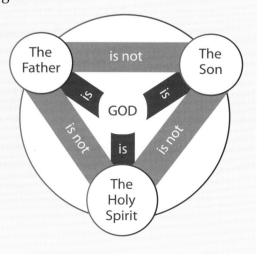

Symbol – The 'triquetra' is a symbolic design sometimes used in Christianity as a Trinitarian symbol. It is possible that it predates Christian beliefs, but the cleverness of its continuous design means it can be interpreted as 'distinction within eternal unity'.

Holy Trinity (Troitsa) by Andrei Rublev (1360–1430).

Icon – Meanwhile, one of the most famous artistic Trinitarian works is that of Andrei Rublev (shown above). Which biblical text is it based on, and what 'features' form part of its theological clues?

🛡 Doctrine Detectives: Clues to the Trinity?

We saw above that in pondering the scriptures, the Church has found 'clues' about the Trinity. Others have found *vestigia trinitatis* – 'footprints' or 'impressions of the Trinity' in nature.

Check out C. S. Lewis: 'You know that in space you can move in three ways – to left or right, backwards or forwards, up or down ... It is something we could never have guessed, and yet, once we have been told, one almost feels one ought to have been able to guess it because it fits in so well with all the things we know already.' C. S. Lewis, *Mere Christianity*

Check out atomic science: The simplest building block of the universe is the hydrogen atom, which has a proton, a neutron and an electron held together in relationship. It is curious to note that the World War II atomic project at Los Alamos was codenamed *Trinity*, but recently scientists have begun exploring whether a 'God-particle' can help explain this atomic unity. Indeed, the 'discovery' of the Higgs boson in 2014 was much celebrated, not least since once and for all it proved that God is a Catholic – because you can't have Mass without it!

OK, so that last line was a tease – but it is intriguing that, independently of religion, scientists are hungry to find the core relationship principle of the universe. So – **can you come up with any 'triune' clues from nature yourself? Why might such things be helpful, and why might such things be considered confusing? Can God's glory or God's nature be known through creation in any case?**

EXCURSUS: Benedict XVI on Trinity and Mission

Benedict XVI: *Deus Caritas Est*, 19

Before Joseph Ratzinger became Pope Benedict XVI he had already spent a lifetime of learned reflection as a leading theologian and through his work at the Vatican Congregation for Doctrine and Faith. In his first encyclical as Pope, he zoomed in on the central message of Christianity – *Deus Caritas Est* – God is Love! In it he explains the significance of belief in the Trinity for a Catholic understanding of mission and evangelism. In section 19 he says:

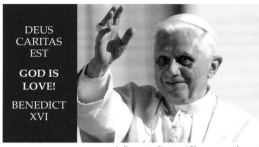

giulio napolitano / Shutterstock.com

'The Spirit is also the energy which transforms the heart of the Church community, so that it becomes a witness before the world to the love of the Father, who wishes to make humanity a single family in his Son.'

- By this, Pope Benedict means that mission comes from the Trinity itself. Pentecost Day is sometimes called the 'birthday of the Church' since it is when the apostles began to preach the Risen Jesus who was 'sent' by the Father and who in turn 'sent' the Spirit.

- This understanding is confirmed by the Catechism: 'The Church on earth is by her nature missionary since, according to the plan of the Father, she has as her origin the mission of the Son and the Holy Spirit' (CCC 850).

- Jesus sent the apostles into the world on a mission! 'Go … and make disciples of all nations, baptising them in the name of the Father and of the Son and of the Holy Spirit, teaching them to observe all that I have commanded you' (Matthew 28:19–20). Baptism is an invitation to humanity to live as a single family within the life of the Trinity, which is love.

Pentecost– St Aloysius' Church, Somers Town, London. Photo / Fr Lawrence Lew OP

Pope Benedict continues:

'The entire activity of the Church is an expression of a love that seeks the integral good of man: it seeks his evangelisation through Word and Sacrament, an undertaking that is often heroic in the way it is acted out in history; and it seeks to promote man in the various arenas of life and human activity.'

- This means that the Church only exists to express the love of the Trinity.

- The Church evangelises by proclaiming the Word of God – her teaching about the life, death, resurrection and ascension of Jesus is the Word of Truth which is 'alive and active' – it cuts through the confusions of humanity 'sharper than a two-edged sword' (see Hebrews 4:12).

- But just as the Word of God became flesh in Jesus, so too the word of God is 'made flesh' in the sacraments of the Church. The invisible God became visible in Jesus of Nazareth. The Church continues the incarnation of Jesus throughout space and time, especially in the proclamation of the Word and the celebration of sacraments.

- To live her evangelising mission faithfully can require great heroism and courage in a world that can sometimes be hostile to the message of love *which is the root of human integrity*. When the Church proclaims that the first human priority is love for God and one another, the world can be indifferent, disdainful or violently hostile. Too often it has other priorities, such as pleasure, power, honour, glory – all things which in excess *disintegrate* not just personalities and families, but entire nations.

'Love is therefore the service that the Church carries out in order to attend constantly to man's sufferings and his needs, including material needs.'

- The Church's whole *raison d'être*, the only reason for her existence, the reason for the Scripture, the Tradition, the Magisterium, the sacraments, the Mass, the popes, the church buildings, church cleaners, altar servers, schools, mother and toddler groups, musicians, flower arrangers, etc. is to get the love of God, the love of the Trinity, flowing through the lives of human beings. The Church is a means to the end of becoming love, becoming holy, becoming like God. Another word for this is a saint. The Church is a saint-making institution.

'The saints are those who have allowed Jesus to get into their boats [i.e. their lives] and who have thereby become not superhuman or angelic but fully human, as alive as God intended them to be.'

Bishop Robert Barron, *Catholicism*, p. 196

- A special task of the Church's evangelising mission is to care for the suffering and the needy. True religion is not only about the next life, but about improving this one too, while never forgetting the next life. The Church has also always encouraged her members to be fully involved in building up a community of love in this life, changing this world for the better – through education, medicine, charity, feeding the hungry, caring for the poor, helping those who are in all kinds of spiritual and physical difficulties.

 Sample Questions

Identification (AO1): Which of the following was NOT a feature of the Baptism of Jesus in the Gospels? The Father / the Son / Mary / the Holy Spirit. (1)

Explanation (AO1): Explain two ways in which belief in the Trinity might be said to be present in Genesis. (4)

Evaluation (AO2): 'Christian Mission can only be understood in the light of the Trinity.' Evaluate this statement, giving arguments to support the statement and arguments from a different point of view. You must refer to Catholic teaching and reach a justified conclusion. (12)

Trinity Understood through Sources of Authority [AQA Spec. B 3.1.3.3]

CORE IDEA

In Unit 3C we explore the Trinity through various sources of authority, in harmony with the typically Catholic way of doing theology through the sources of Scripture, Tradition and Magisterium.

Since in the previous section we have already looked at the Christian understanding of God as a Trinity of persons with reference to the baptism of Jesus (compare Mark 1:9–11 with Matthew 3:16–17 and Galatians 4:6–7), it is wise to examine straight away how in Catholic tradition thinkers from ancient and more recent times have wrestled with this mystery.

Augustine lived from AD 354 to AD 430, and there is a well-known story that one day he was walking on the beach contemplating the mystery of the Trinity when he saw a boy in front of him who had dug a hole in the sand and was going out to the sea again and again and bringing some water to pour into the hole. Augustine asked him, 'What are you doing?' 'I'm going to pour the entire ocean into this hole.' 'That is impossible, the whole ocean will not fit in the hole you have made,' said Augustine. The boy replied, 'And you cannot fit the Trinity in your tiny little brain.' The story concludes by saying that the boy vanished because Augustine had been talking to an angel!

Renata Sedmakova / Shutterstock.com

St Augustine on Trinity and intimacy

In Christian tradition, Augustine is the most influential thinker. He began his career as a professional philosopher and though his mum was Christian, Augustine was a bit wild, Later, looking back in repentance, he admitted having prayed at that time, 'Lord make me chaste but not just yet' (Confessions 8.7). He did father a child whom he called 'Adeodatus' – 'gift of God' but he and his partner never married and eventually separated. Shortly after he dedicated his life to God, Adeodatus too became a Christian but died soon after. Augustine in due course became Bishop of Hippo – a town not too far from present-day Tunis in North Africa. He was absolutely bowled over by the mystery of the Trinity, and this is a tiny extract from his writings:

KEY TERMS

Immanent Trinity = God's innermost being, the inner life of the Triune God.

Economic Trinity = God's outermost expression – how God has revealed Godself in human history.

Perichoresis = A Greek word which tries to describe God's inner life as an eternal interplay of mutual love.

Canon = Another word for Bible – the inspired collection of writings sacred to Christians.

Ecumenical Council = A gathering of all the bishops of the world with the Pope – two examples being: **the Council of Nicaea** in AD 325 and **the Council of Constantinople** in AD 381.

'The Father is not the Son nor the Holy Spirit. To all three belong the same eternity, the same unchangeableness, the same majesty, the same power. In the Father is unity, in the Son equality, in the Holy Spirit the harmony of unity and equality; and these three attributes are all one because of the Father, all equal because of the Son, and all harmonious because of the Holy Spirit.'

On Christian Doctrine, Book 1, Chapter V

Although this is a tightly argued text, Augustine confirms the beliefs and teachings we have been examining:

One God – Father, Son and Holy Spirit share Godness (the qualities listed here are eternity, unchangeableness, majesty and power).

Triune – Father, Son and Holy Spirit are not the same as each other. Each divine person is unique.

God as Love – Each of the three persons gives a gift to the others so that all three persons share that gift:

- The Father gives the gift of unity – unity in the Trinity is a gift or result of the Father.

- The Son gives the gift of equality – equality in the Trinity is a gift or result of the Son.

- The Holy Spirit gives the gift of harmony – harmony in the Trinity is a gift or result of the Holy Spirit.

God for God – Augustine's short extract points out another truth about the *inner life* of the Trinity, or what theologians and scary RE teachers call the *immanent* Trinity. Humanity is not necessary for God to be understood as *love loving*. Believe it or not, God can get through the day without us!

Mission to Pray: Since humanity needs God, not the other way round, God is worthy of human gratitude and praise. This doesn't inflate God's ego, but it helps to deflate ours in a healthy fashion.

Catherine LaCugna on Trinity and intimacy

From a completely different epoch, the second thinker we contemplate is Catherine LaCugna. Although she died at the young age of 44, LaCugna has influenced the way in which modern Catholic thinking emphasises the *outer life* of the Trinity – what theologians and scary RE teachers call the *economic* Trinity. In her famous book *God For Us* published in 1991 she used the metaphor of dance as an image of God's love:

'The divine dance is indeed an apt image of persons in communion ... everything comes from God and everything returns to God, through Christ in the Spirit. This going out and returning is the choreography of the divine dance which takes place from all eternity and is manifest in every moment in creation. There are not two sets of communion – one among the divine persons, the other among human persons ... the one perichoresis, the one mystery of communion includes God and humanity as beloved partners in the dance.'

Catherine LaCugna, *God For Us*, 1991, p. 274

One God – again there are similarities with our studies so far. LaCugna emphasises *communion* – the unity of the divine persons – their *inner* life.

Triune – she uses the image of Father–Son–Spirit *going forth and returning*.

God as Love – in so doing, she emphasises that the Trinity is *love loving* – this is not a static image of what God is like.

God for Us – in contrast to the extract from Augustine, this short extract points out a truth about what theologians and scary RE teachers call the *economic* Trinity. No money is exchanged, only love. LaCugna says that the going forth and returning of this love involves all humanity in a choreography of joy. The Triune God is Lord of the Dance in which we as human beings are invited to join as beloved partners.

Mission to Serve – in imitating God's love, humans become people for others, not just for themselves.

Magisterium, Doctrine and the Councils of the Church

The word 'doctrine' is derived from the Latin word *docta* (which simply means 'things taught'); a *doctrine* is something taught to others by a person with authority to do so.

Just as football coaches pass on their experience, their particular *philosophy*, their *doctrine* about how their sport should be best played to people who want to learn about it, so too the Church's Magisterium passes on wisdom for *life*. This can be done in an *ordinary* everyday sense, but sometimes it comes about in a supreme and solemn way in an Ecumenical (i.e. 'worldwide') Council, which is a gathering of all the bishops of the world together with the Pope. These councils work a bit like the worldwide governing body FIFA, which considers how the *rules* of football are to be interpreted and developed.

Football coach and his team.

'The college of bishops exercises power over the universal Church in a solemn manner in an Ecumenical Council … The infallibility promised to the Church is also present in the body of bishops when, together with Peter's successor [the Pope], they exercise the supreme Magisterium, above all in an Ecumenical Council.' (CCC 884 and 891)

a) The Pope and Apostolic Succession: The connection with St Peter is of supreme importance to Catholics since he was appointed by Jesus to govern the Church (Matthew 16:18–19) – this is why the role of the Pope is so important. Likewise, Jesus promised his apostles that the Spirit would 'lead them into all truth' (John 16:13), and each bishop in the Church can trace his appointment right back to that original group of twelve. This is why the *Magisterium* can claim such authority.

b) Canon – Councils – Creeds: Triple C for Trinity! We have seen that the Church gradually came to understand that God was a Trinity by reflecting on the *Canon*, which is nothing to do with ballistics but is another name for the *books* of the Bible. The word 'God' in the New Testament was understood by the Christian movement as reference to the Father, but Jesus also seemed to be spoken of as 'God' (e.g. Mark 1:9–11; John 1:1–3), and likewise the Holy Spirit (e.g. Mark 1:9–11; Galatians 4:6–7). Over the course of the next three centuries

The Creed of Nicaea (AD 325)

We believe in one God the Father almighty, creator of all things visible and invisible. And in our one Lord Jesus Christ the Son of God, the only begotten born of the Father, that is of the being of the Father, God of God, light of light, true God of true God, born, not made, of one being with the Father, by whom all things were made, which are in heaven and on earth, who for our salvation came down, and became incarnate and was made man, and suffered, and arose again on the third day, and ascended into heaven, and will come to judge the living and the dead. And in the Holy Spirit.

Kiwisoul / Shutterstock.com

the Christian Church reflected on such matters and developed its doctrine of the Trinity. The bishops met in a Council at Nicaea in AD 325 and at another one in Constantinople in AD 381 to produce a Creed – a summary of this belief.

c) Councils are for Clarity – Jesus

One of the useful things about councils is that they clarify matters that have been confusing. The Council of Nicaea in particular clarified that the Son was not inferior to the Father, which is the normal human way of thinking. The Magisterium was pointing out here that when we are dealing with the mystery of God, we are operating outside time – time is part of creation (evening came, morning came, the first day). The Council clarified that the Father could not be 'Father' without the Son already being – the relationship is *co-eternal.*

Councils can be cross! It needs to be said that the debates were heated. St Nicholas (who later gained worldwide fame as Santa niClaus) was suspended for a day after a bust-up with Arius, who insisted that Jesus was *like* the Father but not *the same.* Ultimately the bishops at the Council agreed with St Nicholas and his friend St Athanasius. To emphasise the fact, they censured anyone who, like Arius, said: 'There was [a time] when he was not' and, 'Before he was born, he was not.' The technical term they used for Jesus being *the same* as God was *homoousios* – which is translated as 'of one being', 'of one substance' or 'consubstantial.'

d) Councils are for Clarity – The Holy Spirit

In about AD 360, the same sort of questions that had been raised about the identity of Jesus, the Son of God, were also being asked about the Holy Spirit. Was the Holy Spirit God or not? How was the Holy Spirit related to the Father and the Son, who were fully divine?

Saint Basil was influential in helping sort this problem out, and summarised the Trinity as 'one God or divine reality in the persons of the Father, the Son and the Holy Spirit'.

In 381 the Emperor Theodosius called a Council at Constantinople. It reaffirmed the Creed of Nicaea from 325, but expanded it a little to underline that the Holy Spirit was also fully God and is professed every Sunday in Catholic churches and in many other churches too. The main additions concern the Holy Spirit and the understanding of the Church.

The Creed of Nicaea–Constantinople (AD 381)

We believe... in the Holy Spirit, the Lord, the giver of life, who proceeds from the Father, who together with the Father and Son is worshipped and glorified, who spoke through the prophets. And in one holy, catholic, and apostolic Church. We confess one baptism for the forgiveness of sins. We look for the resurrection of the dead, and the life of eternity to come. Amen.

Memory Moment

Quiz

- What is the Magisterium?

- What is an Ecumenical Council? Can you name two such councils?

- What is a creed?

- What is a doctrine?

- Who was Arius and what did he believe?

- Which two men with names beginning with the letters 'N' and 'A' opposed Arius?

- What did they believe?

- What did Basil the Great teach about the Trinity?

🛡 Doctrine Detectives

From the short extracts provided, how many similarities and differences can you find between what St Augustine said and what Catherine LaCugna said about the Trinity?

 Sample Questions

Identification and Explanation (AO1): Give two reasons why the Magisterium has authority for Catholics. (2)

Explanation (AO1): Explain two features of St Augustine's understanding of the Trinity. (4)

Evaluation (AO2): 'The only way that Christians know about the Trinity is because it was taught by the Early Councils.' Evaluate this statement, giving arguments to support the statement and arguments from a different point of view. You must refer to Catholic teaching and reach a justified conclusion. (12)

Trinity in Catholic Faith and Practice [AQA Spec. B 3.1.3.4]

In Unit 3D we explore the Trinity through the practices of the Church:

i. The meaning and importance of baptism as a sign of initiation and participation in the life of God, Father, Son and Spirit.

ii. The significance of prayer as a 'raising of the heart and mind to God', including contrasting features of traditional and spontaneous prayers.

iii. How prayer and posture are linked in Christian worship.

Baptism as Sacrament of Initiation and sharing the life of the Trinity

A sacrament is a ritual (a religious ceremony) performed in the life of the Church in order to continue Jesus' sanctifying work of love in the world.

To be a fully initiated member of the Catholic Church, a person must receive three sacraments – Baptism, Confirmation and Eucharist. These three sacraments 'lay the foundations of every Christian life … The faithful [i.e. the members of the Church] are born anew by Baptism, strengthened by the Sacrament of Confirmation, and receive in the Eucharist the food of eternal life' (CCC 1212).

'Baptism' comes from the Greek word *baptizein*, meaning to plunge or immerse. The immersion into water or the pouring of water over a person's head is a sign that symbolises three things:

○ The water is a *cleansing* – it washes away original sin.

○ The water is a *burial* – the person 'disappears under water' to symbolise a kind of burial which imitates Christ's death.

○ The water is *new life* – the person experiences rebirth like Christ's resurrection – and is given a name, a new identity in the love of the Trinity – in the name of the Father, Son and Spirit.

KEY TERMS

Sacrament = A Church ritual which continues Jesus' work of love in the world.

Baptism = The sacramental gateway into the life of the Trinity and the Church.

Prayer = The raising of one's mind and heart to God, consciously making time to be with God, to remember that all of life is lived in God's presence.

Types of prayer = Adoration, thanksgiving, repentance, intercession, petition.

Prayer: raising mind and heart to God

Prayer is described in the *Catechism of the Catholic Church* (CCC 2559) as 'the raising of one's mind and heart to God'.

- Christians believe that every moment of life is lived in the presence of God, for 'in Him we live and move and have our being' (Acts 17:28).

- Prayer involves setting aside even just a moment of time to 'tune into' the eternal wavelength of the Trinitarian God who gave us life and who will be there when this life fails us.

- The Church believes that the important thing about prayer is not *how* you do it, but *that* you do it. Taking a dogmatic decision not to pray is like having the TV or radio on standby and refusing to even try switching it on.

- Even devout Christians worry about what prayer is and how to do it. Should it be done with words, without words, using music, reading scripture, thinking thoughts or images, trying to empty the mind of thoughts and images? The answer, of course, is to use anything that is helpful.

Cardinal Basil Hume (1923–99) once said in a retreat he gave in Rome, 'The only important thing about prayer is that you show up to do it! That you say to God, "Lord, this time is yours. Do with this time what you want – whether I end up happy, sad, worried, bored, concentrating on my sore back or looking at my watch – this time is yours!"'

Bronze statue of Cardinal Basil Hume outside St Mary's Roman Catholic Cathedral, Newcastle.
© Copyright Stephen McKay

Common themes in prayer

CCC 2626–2643 lists five major themes or purposes when someone prays, all of which are done during Mass:

Adoration: The simple acknowledgement by human beings that God is God. It is acknowledging the glory that belongs to the Trinitarian God alone. Mass begins and ends in the name of the Father, Son and Spirit.

Thanksgiving: We only live and love because of God. 'Eucharist' is the Greek word for thanksgiving, and so Mass is also a huge 'thank you' to God for everything.

Repentance: An expression of sorrow for our failings to be all we can be. This type of prayer is done in the Penitential Rite at the beginning of Mass.

Intercession: Prayers in which people ask God for things on *behalf* of other people who are in some sort of need. At Mass the Bidding Prayers or Prayer of the Faithful are examples of intercessory prayer.

Petition: We all need things in life, and so we should not be afraid to ask God for things we need.

Traditional prayer and spontaneous prayer

Prayer that is prayed aloud can use words and formulas that draw on the many centuries of wisdom in the Church's long tradition of prayer (e.g. the Our Father, the Hail Mary, the Glory Be, the Rosary) – this is traditional prayer.

> In contrast, prayer can be more informal and spontaneous, when a person uses their own words without preparation (sometimes called *extempore* ['out of the moment'] prayer).

It is entirely apt on the one hand for a Christian to use other people's words in prayer – just as humans borrow their parents' language while learning to make it their own.

> On the other hand, a believer has to give prayer their own stamp, the mark of their own life, joy, laughter, tears and heartache. The words can't just be parroted without mindfulness or feeling.

Saying is not Praying: The challenge for the Christian believer, whether they use formal or informal prayers, is to *pray* prayers, not just *say* prayers. Jesus was not too keen on vacuous vapouring, especially in public (Matthew 6:7).

> Instead, he tells his followers to do the opposite – to pray in secret and meet the Father in the intimacy of their own heart (Matthew 6:6). Moreover, Jesus constantly chose solitude in his life of prayer and used silence at crucial moments (e.g. Luke 6:12–13, Matthew 14:23 and 27:14), for the deepest of truths must be pondered in the heart (see Mary in Luke 2:19).

Posture in prayer

When we are praying, we can express our worship and love of the Triune God by the movements and position of our body. This is a non-verbal way of communicating our attitudes towards God. Some common postures are:

- **Standing:** this was the normal attitude of Jews adopted by the early Christians, and was seen as a sign of honouring God. Christians also saw in standing an acknowledgement of the Risen (and therefore standing) Jesus.

- **Kneeling:** this signifies adoration; or humility before the glory/ greatness of God; or sorrow; or penance. The genuflection (in which the knee of one leg touches the ground near the ankle of the other leg) is also a sign of adoration or honour, especially before the Blessed Sacrament when it is present in a church.

- **Prostration:** this is lying down flat on the ground, face down. It is a sign of complete obedience before God, utter abandonment to God's will (it happens when a man is ordained as a priest).

- **Sitting:** the posture of someone presiding at an act of worship (e.g. the priest at Mass); it is also a sign of the authority to teach. Sitting is also a posture that allows a congregation to be more relaxed during readings and sermons.

Memory Moment

P is for **P**rayer, the lifeblood or **P**ulse of every believer

R is for the **R**aising of mind and heart to God

A is for **A**doration, worship, praise, recognising the glory of God

Y is for **Y**OU. Prayers can't be empty – *you* are the main ingredient – you may have flashy words, faltering words or even no words, but just by raising your hands you can offer a prayer to God.

🛡 Denial Detectives

Most, if not all, people will have prayed a prayer for something and felt that prayer has not been answered. C. S. Lewis, however, once said that we will probably spend a lot of time in Heaven thanking God for those prayers of ours to which God replied, 'No!' It is also sometimes said that 'Wait – not just yet' is just as much an answer to a prayer as 'Yes'.

Is C. S. Lewis just making the most of his disappointment or can you think of examples of such situations? Can you think of reasons why God might not want to grant somebody's request, at least for the time being?

(Q) Sample Questions

Identification (AO1): Which of the following is a sacrament of initiation? Baptism/Anointing of the Sick/Marriage/Adoration. (1)

Explanation (AO1): Explain how two different postures reflect contrasting Christian views on prayer. (4)

Evaluation (AO2): 'Christians should only use traditional prayers, not spontaneous prayers.' Evaluate this statement, giving arguments to support the statement and arguments from a different point of view. You must refer to Catholic teaching and reach a justified conclusion. (12)

Redemption and Forms of Expression [AQA Spec 3.1.4.1]

CORE IDEA

The main aim of this section is to understand how the architecture of Catholic churches is designed to help believers 'experience' the mystery of redemption celebrated in Mass. Having mastered the basics, students will then be able to spot differences in architectural designs and see what aspect of belief is being emphasised in particular Catholic and non-Catholic churches.

Redemption overview

° The focus of this unit on redemption is the mystery of salvation – sometimes called the paschal mystery. Why is it called that?

° 'Paschal' comes from the Hebrew Pesach, meaning 'Passover'.

° Just as Israel was miraculously saved from slavery and death in Egypt following the sacrifice of a lamb partaken in a sacred meal, so Catholics believe that it is the sacrifice of Jesus and the partaking of the Eucharist which makes present the miracle of deliverance from the slavery of sin and the power of death.

° For this reason the Mass is understood as 'the source and summit' of the Christian life, and it is an example of an enacted prayer, which is at the heart of Catholic practice.

° This sacred importance is emphasised by the Sunday obligation for Catholics to attend Mass once a week on the Lord's Day.

As a consequence:

a) The architecture of churches is designed to express this central drama of redemption which is enacted in the liturgy – through the positioning of the altar, the lectern and so forth.

b) The beliefs and teachings of the Church also underpin the ritual – they remind the faithful of the significance of events such as the death, resurrection and ascension of Jesus.

c) The sources of authority confirm in different ways the power and poetry of the story of redemption and how conscience involves every human being in the drama of sin and salvation.

d) The practices of the Church: Catholic understanding of the Mass as a saving meal is not merely symbolic. Catholics believe that the Body of Christ is really present in two especial ways – in the people gathered by God in love, and in the sacramental bread and wine transformed in love by God.

Part 1   The church itself

- **Prayers in stone:** There is little doubt that Christian churches, abbeys, cathedrals and minsters rank among the most wonderful and beautiful buildings in the world. In Europe, the single most visited place is a church – Notre Dame in Paris. Likewise in London, St Paul's, Westminster Abbey and Westminster Cathedral have millions of visitors, and Rome too is full of famous churches, especially St Peter's. Such places have long been called 'prayers in stone' because their design and craftsmanship do what prayer does – 'raise the heart and mind towards God'.

- **Church without churches:** The big mistake that can be made, however, is that people can think that churches are the Church. No! Take a look at the painting here by Elizabeth Wang. The Church is first of all *the people of God* understood as *the Body of Christ*. For many centuries it was basically illegal to be a Christian in the Roman Empire; there were no special buildings, and the believers gathered in homes and even underground in catacombs to worship God. Church without churches? No problem.

Christ among his people by Elizabeth Wang

- **Public place for Eucharist:** After Emperor Constantine in AD 312 it became possible to build public places for Christian worship. At that point, Christian celebration of *the mysteries* of redemption became public and churches were designed to facilitate the celebration of Eucharist.

- **East is east?** Quite quickly, it became common for churches to be literally *orientated* – i.e. with the altar towards the eastern side, – though the precise motives are uncertain:

  - The East is where the sun rises, and the people often gathered for Eucharist at dawn.
  - The rising sun also symbolised the resurrection of Jesus conquering the darkness.
  - Christianity had Jewish roots – most believers facing east would worship facing Jerusalem.

Part 2   The essential elements

Key features: From the earliest times it appears that the main ingredients of the church included the altar, the lectern, the tabernacle and the cross, all of which point to redemption.

The altar and redemption: The altar occupies the focal point of a church and has two meanings:

- **Altar of sacrifice:** First, it is the place of offering of bread and wine by the people and of the redemptive sacrifice of Jesus. In this way it calls to mind the ancient tradition of Israel whereby the people offered animals to God as a sacrifice for sins. In the Christian tradition this is no longer necessary because God has made the sacrifice instead in Jesus – the Lamb of God – who said: 'This is my body which will be given up for you.'

- **Table of the Eucharist:** Second, it is the place of redemptive nourishment, of food for the journey. In this way it especially calls to mind the Last Supper. Jesus did not give the disciples a list of things to say, he gave them a prayer ritual of bread and wine to enact and said: 'Do this in memory of me.' For this reason, the altar is sometimes called 'the table of the Eucharist', or *mensa* – which is Latin for 'table'.

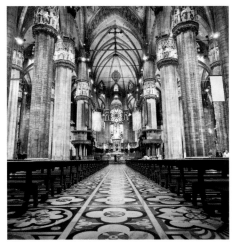

High Altars and Side Altars: The numerous side chapels and altars at which priests will also celebrate Mass are a feature of bigger churches. These are distinguished from the main or 'high' altar, which will often have a covering structure of some kind to emphasise its importance.

Altar Stones and Relics: Over the centuries it became traditional for even wooden altars to have an inset piece of stone and for that in turn to have an inlaid relic from a Christian saint of the Church. Normally a fragment of bone, it is meant to be inspirational rather than morbid! It is a way in which the gathered believers – the communion of saints on earth in Eucharist – are uniting themselves with the 'communion of saints' in heaven.

Lectern and redemption:

- The lectern is the place where the Holy Scriptures are proclaimed. Sometimes this is to one side of the altar, though it can be placed facing the altar if the congregation seating is in 'choir' – arranged either side of both.

- Lecterns can be very simple or very grand. A common lectern decoration has the four symbols of the Gospel writers – the winged man for Matthew, the winged lion for Mark, the winged ox for Luke, and an eagle for John – often acting as the plinth on which is placed ...

- ... the *lectionary*, which is a special arrangement of scripture readings used through the year for the various festivals and saints' days.

- The lectern represents redemption since it is understood in Catholic churches to be 'the table of the word'. Jesus replied to Satan during his temptation that 'Man does not live by bread alone but by every word that comes from the mouth of God' (Matthew 4:4). Jesus is the Divine Word and his saving message is *received* by the believer from the lectern.

Tabernacle and redemption

Catholic churches in regular use will always have a *tabernacle* – a secure ornamental cabinet made of precious metal or bespoke carpentry.

This will normally be placed on a plinth to the side of the altar, but frequently in older churches it may be set *into* an altar, and in rare instances even be suspended above the altar.

The tabernacle contains the Blessed Sacrament. For Catholics, the Eucharistic bread consecrated during Mass is ultra-special, a presence par excellence of Christ among us – hence its other name, 'Holy Communion'.

StockPhotosArt / Shutterstock.com

To emphasise the sacred nature of the Blessed Sacrament, the tabernacle will have a lighted candle or 'sanctuary lamp' nearby.

'Tabernacle' simply means 'tent', which deliberately calls to mind aspects of the Jewish roots of Christianity – the notion of *Shekinah* – God's abiding presence among the people (Exodus 25:8) – and the Ark of the Covenant being placed in a tent (Exodus 40:21).

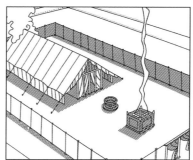

To further emphasise this 'tent' symbolism, the tabernacle may well be covered with a special veil or ornate cloth.

For Catholics, the tabernacle thus symbolises redemption, that God is with us, and God's *Real Presence* among his people is brought about through the Eucharist – the saving ritual of the Mass.

Crucifix and redemption

Normally in Catholic churches there will also be a prominent depiction of the crucifixion – either a cross or a painting of the scene on Calvary.

The symbolism of this is to remind believers of the sacrifice of Jesus by which redemption is accomplished. No longer are they separated from God because of their sins – Jesus the Lamb of God has reunited God and humanity through his sacrifice of love.

In modern churches, sculptors sometimes depict a risen rather than a crucified Christ on the cross. This too symbolises redemption, emphasising the triumph of Jesus over death.

Memory Moment

The key features of a Catholic church are:

Altar

Lectern

Tabernacle

All signs of

Redemption

Design Detectives

Knowing the basics of church design, it can be intriguing to see how they differ and why. Match up the descriptions with the explanations:

Cross shape: As the centuries unfolded, cross-shaped design became another common feature of churches such that the architecture of the church called to mind the death of Jesus.	A. To convey this sense of the redemptive mystery, the altar is actually hidden behind a highly decorated screen, or iconostasis.
Round shape: Church architects in later periods, particularly the latter part of the twentieth century, wanted to emphasise the sense of Mass as a redemptive meal.	B. Alongside older buildings such as St Paul's, there are intriguing newer cathedrals such as Coventry which set aspects of redemption in a modern context. Another has an installation by the controversial artist Tracey Emin – which one is it, and what did she do?
Protestant churches: As noted above, the main Protestant traditions went in the other direction, and Evangelical, Calvinist, Baptist and Methodist churches have very simple undecorated interiors.	C. Since people were lined up in rows gazing at the ritual action unfolding before them, it tended to further emphasise the sense of redemptive sacrifice.
Eastern churches: Among Eastern Orthodox churches the architecture began to reflect the sense that the Eucharist was a divine action, a redemptive heavenly liturgy.	D. The centrepiece of such churches will often either be the lectern or the pulpit rather than the altar, which mirrors their emphasis on the Word of God rather than on the sacraments as the means to salvation.
National styles: In Catholic churches, sharp-pointed features of 'Gothic' architecture and an emphasis on stonework are a strong tradition in England and northern Europe, whereas in Italy and Spain architecture is more rounded and internally pictorial.	E. One way of doing this was to make sure people were 'gathered around' – literally – in a huge circular arrangement. A famous example of this is Liverpool's Cathedral of Christ the King.
Anglican churches: Although greatly influenced by the Protestant tradition, the Church of England has largely retained the 'prayer in stone' sense of architecture partly because it is the custodian of such a large number of older churches, minsters and cathedrals which were part of the larger Catholic heritage.	F. Spain has some particularly imaginative basilicas, none more so than La Sagrada Familia in Barcelona. The architect, Antoni Gaudí, wanted to create a church that felt like nature was reaching up in praise of God. Arguably his wonderful use of colour, curves, light and creation captures the sense of redemption as effectively as anywhere else on earth.

Q **Sample Questions**

Identification (AO1): What is a lectern? (1)

Identification (AO1): Identify two symbolic features represented by a tabernacle. (2)

Explanation (AO1): Explain two ways in which the position of the altar helps the faithful to worship. Refer to Catholic teaching in your answer. (5)

Evaluation (AO2): 'Christian churches are all the same.' Evaluate this statement. In your answer you should give developed arguments to support the statement and arguments to support a different point of view. You should refer to Catholic teaching and reach a justified conclusion. (12)

La Sagrada Familia, Barcelona, Spain.
Huang Zheng / Shutterstock.com

Redemption in Beliefs and Teaching [AQA Spec 3.1.4.2]

CORE IDEA

The main theme in this unit is how redemption can be understood as a massive act of restoration on the part of God. The death, resurrection and ascension of Jesus are at the heart of this. These actions have restored broken humanity, and Catholics believe that Mass is a commemoration of and participation in that saving mystery.

The death, resurrection and ascension: significance in the story of redemption

The Death of Jesus is extensively recorded in all the Gospels. It is the first part of what is called the *paschal* mystery. To repeat, 'Paschal' comes from the Hebrew *Pesach*, meaning 'Passover'. Just as Israel was miraculously *saved* from slavery and death in Egypt following the sacrifice of a lamb, the understanding is that the sacrifice of Jesus as *the Lamb of God* redeems believers from the slavery of sin and the power of death and reunites humanity with God. It is sometimes called *the atonement*, which literally means *at-one-ment*.

The Cross is rich in meaning for Christians today.

° **Consolation:** Death brings life, a sorrow brings gladness.

° **Reconciliation:** Jesus' forgiving means that a sign of desolation becomes a sign of reconciliation.

° **Suffering:** Persecuted Christians today derive great encouragement from the example of Jesus' own suffering.

° **Belonging:** This act of love challenges the natural human fear of abandonment. The veil of the Temple is torn in two because now there is no longer a separation between humanity and God.

Contrasting view: The death of Jesus is just a human tragedy which often happens to free thinkers. There is nothing divine in cruel execution. Jesus had clearly upset the religious authorities, hence they were agitated, but it was a political act on the part of the Romans, who were anxious to quash any unrest.

The Resurrection report is also featured in all the Gospel accounts. The various accounts concur on key details. The women who went to anoint the body of Jesus found the stone rolled away and the tomb empty. Since in that culture women were not considered reliable witnesses it is astonishing that the Gospel accounts would emphasise this fact. The doubt of the disciples is not glossed over, nor the theory that someone had stolen the body. Ultimately, the apparitions of Jesus confirm the disciples in their faith and the Good News is proclaimed.

KEY TERMS

Lamb of God = A title given to Jesus in the Gospels.

Paschal Mystery = This comes from the Hebrew *Pesach* – meaning Passover.

Passover = The moment when the Angel of Death 'passed over' the houses of the Hebrews, sparing their firstborn.

Grace = The free gift of God's love.

Redemption = The way in which Jesus has reconciled humanity to God – sometimes referred to as *salvation* or *atonement*.

Salvation = God's rescuing of humanity from sin.

The Resurrection is rich in meaning for Christians today.

- **Consolation:** The resurrection is the ultimate sign of consolation for Christians in the face of the sorrow and loss. As Paul says: 'Death where is your victory, death where is your sting!' (1 Corinthians 15:55).

- **New Life:** A place of tears becomes a place of joy, a place that is empty fills the earth with hope. So funerals and graveyards are marked by flowers to celebrate faith in a new, eternal life.

- **Good News:** A place of silence becomes a place of proclamation. Just as the women rather than the disciples were first to tell of the resurrection, so *every Christian* is called to proclaim the Good News.

> **Contrasting view:** The bodily resurrection of Jesus is too good to be true. No one claims to have seen it happen, so either the body was stolen, the execution was botched or the disciples had some kind of communal hallucination and thought it was an apparition. It is easier to believe the soul can survive death – a body being raised is too far-fetched.

The Ascension is recorded by St Luke in the Acts of the Apostles after a classic '40-day' period of *transformation* which changes everything. It is not a random add-on whereby Jesus disappears like James Bond on a jet-pack – 'the ascension is essential' as the culmination of the work of Christ on earth and his heavenly return to God the Father *from whence he shall come to judge the living and the dead.* The last scene in Matthew's Gospel has similarities when Jesus promises to be with the disciples always (28:20), as does John 14:19: 'The world will not see me but you will see me.' The risen body of Christ becomes *hidden* from sight while *believers*, who are to understand themselves as the body of Christ, become more *visible*.

The Ascension is rich in meaning for Christians today.

- **Consolation:** 'I am with you always' – Jesus *leaves* but promises to be *with* his followers *for all time*.

- **Building the Kingdom:** The rupture between heaven and earth is ended. The Son of Man *exalted* as Christ the King calls on the sons of men to build with *humility* the Kingdom *on earth as it is in heaven*.

- **The Body of Christ:** Christ *returns* to God while the disciples return to their earthly task – instead of just gawping into the sky, Christians are called to serve as Jesus served – to be the Body of Christ: 'He has no hands but yours.'

- **Judgement:** Christians are aware of Final Judgement but are given hope that the One entrusted with authority *to judge* is the One who pleads *mercy* for humanity in the Court of the Almighty.

- **Christ's Return:** The Ascension contains the promise of Christ's triumphant return – the Second Coming.

> **Contrasting view:** The Ascension account seems a bit confused since Luke and Matthew seem to disagree on the location. It is not as important as the Resurrection and was probably just a way of saying that the apparitions ended at some point. Also the idea that Heaven is above us and Hell below seems a bit simplistic even for believers nowadays.

Differing Christian views on salvation and grace

Meditation on these mysteries has led to three main views on how someone is saved:

Totally down to God – Original sin has rendered humanity a hopeless case. Only *grace* – the utter free gift of God's love – can do the restoration job; the task of the human being is simply to accept this in order to be saved. This is sometimes called 'justification by faith' and is often associated with Martin Luther (1483–1546). In terms of timing, salvation for the believer has already happened, an emphasis found in many Protestant Churches. The main problem is that it is often linked to the idea held by followers of John Calvin (1509–64) that believers are *pre-destined* by God to be saved, which is rejected by most Christians.

Totally down to believers – The *Imago Dei* and free will have rendered humanity capable of choosing good or evil. Believers are responsible for their actions and can reach holiness by their own efforts. This is sometimes called 'justification by works' and is associated with a British theologian, Pelagius (AD 354–420). In terms of timing, salvation is almost a future target to be achieved. No particular Church is associated with it nowadays because the main problem is that if we can save ourselves, there is no need for Christ's incarnation or redemptive actions.

Totally down to both – Despite original sin, humanity can participate in 'god-filled'/'graced' actions, whether they be sacraments or acts of kindness, and can 'die to sin' through self-giving. In other words, humanity cooperates – literally 'co-works' – with God through grace in the mystery of salvation. This is sometimes associated with eastern Christian thinkers such St Athanasius (AD 296–373), but it is widely shared. In terms of timing, salvation is begun by Christ and continues by grace through life, but is only fulfilled in heaven. The Catholic and Orthodox Churches have this belief, as do many Anglicans.

🛡 Mass Detectives

The story of redemption has directly influenced the Mass, which is the central worship act (liturgy) of Catholic Christianity. The Mass *re-presents* – 'makes present' – the mystery of Redemption outlined in the Memory Moment on the next page. Can you follow the clues from those seven boxes to sort out the Mass in its proper *order* in the list below?

i. The reading from the Old Testament: listening to the story of salvation.

ii. The Eucharistic Liturgy: the offering of the bread and wine and commemoration of the Last Supper and the sacrifice of Jesus.

iii. The Rite of Penance/Sorrow for sin: the believers acknowledge that they have not lived up to being made in God's image.

iv. The Dismissal: the believers do not stay gazing at God or at each other for ever. They are sent forth, renewed in the image of God to renew the earth with His love. This is the *Missa* – the sending forth – from which Mass gets its name.

v. In the name of the Father, Son and Holy Spirit: the believers are gathered and reminded that they are in the God-zone!

vi. The reading from the Gospel: listening to the life of the God-man, Jesus.

vii. The Communion Rite: the Body of Christ (made up of the believers) receives the immortal Body of Christ (really present in the sacrament). The Bread of Life restores the faithful to communion, in love, with each other and God.

Memory Moment

Redemption as restoration through the death, resurrection and ascension of Jesus.
Redemption can be understood as a massive act of restoration on the part of God which Jesus brings about through his **death**, **resurrection** and **ascension**.

It is perhaps best represented in diagram form, showing the seven different phases whereby broken humanity is restored to its glorious destiny:

RESTORATION — By his wounds you have been healed

THE COSMIC ORDER
As the final act of the Cosmic Creation, God says: 'Let us make humanity in our own image.' (Genesis 1:26)

ASCENSION RESTORES COSMIC ORDER
Jesus ASCENDS to sit at the *right hand* of God – the place of cosmic power and authority. A *SON OF MAN* is now worthy – like unto GOD (see Daniel 7:13–14). Humanity will be judged with mercy.

FALLEN CREATION
Adam disobeys and tries to become God-like. The relationships of God to Man, Woman to Man, and Man to Creation are all compromised, and Adam and Eve are denied access to the Tree of Life. (Genesis 3:1–24)

RESURRECTION AND RECREATION
The day after Sabbath, Jesus, the New Adam, is raised in a *garden*. It is the first day of a New Creation witnessed by *a woman*. Jesus' obedience repairs the sin of Adam. Immortality is restored. The Tree of Death (the Cross) becomes the Tree of Life.

RITUAL SACRIFICE
Through the long story of salvation, the Chosen People try to atone for their sinfulness, but their offerings through sacrifices in the Temple are to no avail.

JESUS' DEATH AS THE ONE SACRIFICE
Jesus puts an end to animal offerings in the Temple as *the Lamb of God* who offers himself as a sacrifice for the sins of humanity. This is known as atonement – the *at-one-ment* of God and humanity.

RECONCILIATION THROUGH THE GOD-MAN
Ultimately the only answer seemed to be for God to become human and *show* humanity how life should be lived. Inevitably this would be characterised by *sacrifice*. Jesus said: 'Greater love has no one than to lay down their life for their friends.' (John 15:13)

Q Sample Questions

Definition (AO1): What are 'grace', 'salvation', and 'redemption'? (1)

Explanation (AO1): Explain two ways in which Christ is understood to have restored creation to its proper order. (4)

Evaluation (AO2): 'The Ascension is of little importance for Christians today.' Evaluate this statement. In your answer you should give developed arguments to support the statement and arguments to support a different point of view. You should refer to Catholic teaching and reach a justified conclusion. (12)

Redemption and Sources of Authority [AQA Spec 3.1.4.3]

CORE IDEA

This section explores in more detail just how the sources of authority confirm in different ways the power and poetry of the story of redemption and how conscience involves every human being in the drama of sin and salvation.

Scripture

A more detailed reading of the scriptures will help in memorising the meaning and significance of the key moments in the mystery of redemption. Purely to help in the memory task, the accounts have been schematized in a threefold manner as humiliation, confusion and revelation. Note that witness is a theme linking each episode in the drama of redemption.

Death of Jesus in Mark 15:21–39

All the Gospels have long passages devoted to the story of Jesus' death, and as an example, the crucifixion is described by Mark in Chapter 15, verses 21–39.

○ **The Humiliation** of Jesus is emphasised, which fits with the picture of God's holy servant prophesied in Isaiah 53. He needs help to carry the cross; he is taken to Golgotha, the 'skull-strewn' place of execution; he is offered a painkiller of wine and myrrh; he is stripped naked; soldiers play dice for his clothes; he is crucified with two thieves who, along with the religious authorities and passers-by, mock him (verses 21–32).

○ **The Confusion:** at noon, a darkness falls for 3 hours which symbolises a de-creation – a quenching of the light of God – and the fear, despair and confusion of humanity (see Genesis 1:3). Jesus cries *Eloi Eloi* – 'My God, My God' – but the people nearby think he is shouting for *Eliyah* – Elijah the Prophet – and they wait to see if he will come to Jesus' help (verses 33–36).

○ **The Revelation:** Jesus is actually quoting Psalm 22, which starts in despair but ends in the cosmic triumph of God's servant (check it out!). He breathes his last and immediately the veil of the Temple which covers the Holy of Holies is torn in two, symbolising that the ultimate sacrifice has been made and humanity is no longer separate from God. What his own people and even his own disciples struggle to realise, the pagan centurion sees revealed and it is he who acts as *witness*: 'Truly, this man was God's Son!' (verses 34–39).

KEY TERMS

Ascension = Jesus' return to the Heavenly Father.

Pentecost = Comes from '50' and was a special harvest feast which took place fifty days after Passover and commemorated the giving of the Law to Moses.

Recapitulation = A redemption theory associated with St Irenaeus.

Satisfaction = A redemption theory associated with St Anselm.

Conscience = The inner moral compass of human beings.

Resurrection in John 20:1–18

The Resurrection account in John is notable for some particular redemption themes.

- **The Humiliation:** The whole point of John's Gospel is to become a witness to Jesus, and in his account, it is explicit that the first witness to the empty tomb is not a disciple, still less Peter, the leader of the group who denied even knowing Jesus during his trial. No, it is a *woman*, Mary Magdalene, who discovers the scene and who rushes off to tell the disciples (verses 1–3).

- **The Confusion:** Peter runs with John to the tomb, but even then he is second in the foot race! Worse, he doesn't understand what has happened, and Mary too is very confused, convinced that the body of Jesus has been stolen. Intriguingly, John emphasises that it is *the Beloved Disciple* who understands – as if love is what cuts through the confusion to faith and to hope (verses 4–10).

- **The Revelation:** In a lovely way, the Gospel then returns the reader to Eden, by means of a risen man, a fallen woman and a garden! Mary Magdalene turns round and asks someone she thinks is the gardener if he has taken the body. Jesus is the new man, like Adam, a gardener, but an *obedient* son of God, representing a New Creation, a new immortal humanity. He calls her by name: 'Mary' and she cries out *Rabbuni* – 'My Lord!' Mary represents our fallen nature, but now, named in love, she becomes the one who proclaims the life giving word of God – the first *witness* to see the Risen Lord. Last but not least, the tragic garden, like the earth, is also renewed. From being a tragic place of lost immortality, it now becomes a place which symbolises life, joy and communion with God (vv.11-18).

Ascension – Acts 1:6–11

Luke has taken care to mention that the period following the Resurrection and the Ascension is 40 days – a period of transformation, so things are about *to change* (1:3).

- **The Humiliation:** It is clear that, for the disciples, they are still looking for a gesture of power that will establish an earthly kingdom – or at least they want to have a clue as to when it will happen. Jesus tells them they are not to know times and dates but commends them to seek the power of the Spirit instead *so that they will be witnesses* to the ends of the earth (verses 6–8).

- **The Confusion:** Jesus is then 'lifted up' – while this symbolises the exaltation of Jesus as God's Son (see Psalm 2), the thought of Jesus leaving them would be discombobulating for the disciples. Jesus is then covered by the 'I AM Cloud' – while this symbolises the presence of God (see the story of Exodus 13:21 and the Transfiguration in Luke 9:34–35), it also depicts the limitations of human understanding in the face of the mystery of God (verse 9).

- **The Revelation:** The apostles suddenly become aware of two men clothed in white. In Jewish thinking, two was the number necessary for proper *witness*, and their shining robes indicate that they are the angelic messengers from Luke 24:4 who announced the Resurrection. 'Angel' means messenger, and they duly get the disciples back 'on message': the disciples are not to stay gawping up to heaven – in due time Jesus will return as they have seen him depart. This seals the revelation that Jesus is at the right hand of God and will return as the cosmic ruler of all, the Son of Man prophesied in Daniel 7:14. Things are different now and there is the task of witness at hand – see Luke 18:8.

Pentecost – Acts 2:1–4

The witness theme that links the redemption events together is completed in the story of Pentecost.

- **The Humiliation:** The scene Luke depicts in Acts is that the disciples were gathered in prayer. They are in an upper room – perhaps too scared to go out (Acts 1:13/2:1). After all, their leader had been killed – why would they be treated differently to him?

- **The Confusion:** Clearly God had other ideas and seems to make it too dangerous to stay inside! Fire and windstorm are classic signs of *theophany* – a 'God moment' or *manifestation* which normally causes panic – imagine if your classmates suddenly had pyros flying out of their heads (verses 2–3)!

- **The Revelation:** Suddenly the meaning emerges. The tongues of fire mean the apostles will have the courage *to witness* openly. Moreover, at Babel, humanity tried to build a tower to heaven to 'be like God', and to foil humanity, their languages were confused by divine command (Genesis 11:1–9). Now, at Pentecost, God instead comes to earth and humanity is renewed in God's image through the Spirit. No more confusion, no more disunity, for the Spirit bestows the gift of tongues so that the apostles can *witness* to the entire human race (verse 4).

Memory Moment

Complete the table

REDEMPTION – THE PATTERN OF WITNESS IN SCRIPTURE				
	Humiliation	Confusion	Revelation 1	Revelation 2
Death	Cross – naked			
Resurrection			The New Adam	
Ascension		The I __ Cloud		
Pentecost				Babel – Tongues

Meditating upon the mystery of redemption down the ages, different thinkers have emphasised different images or *metaphors* for it. Two of the most famous are from Irenaeus, who died in AD 202, and Anselm (1033–1109).

Irenaeus: Restoration by Recapitulation:

- Irenaeus emphasises what Jesus **was** as the *perfect human:*
- The problem with humanity was that Adam had blown it – he'd lost the plot – and everyone was compromised by that disobedience.
- The incarnation *redeems* this disastrous situation … Jesus 'commenced afresh the long line of human beings … so that what we had lost in Adam – namely, to be according to the image and likeness of God – we might recover in Christ Jesus.'
- 'In His work of *recapitulation*, Christ summed up all things … in order that, as our species went down to death through a vanquished man, so we may ascend to life again through a victorious one' (*Adversus Haereses*, 3.18.1 and 5.21.1).

Anselm: Restoration by Satisfaction:

- Anselm emphasises what Jesus **did** as the *perfect sacrifice*:
- Anselm was reacting against a theory which suggested that the sin of humanity meant that Satan held all souls captive and that he had to be paid off. In this thinking, Jesus is the *ransom* to end the cosmic kidnap!
- Anselm thought it bonkers for God to owe Satan anything, but the problem was more that all *humanity* had dishonoured God. Somehow, an equal gesture of honour had to put things right – the moral cosmos was out of balance – but how could such an amazing *redemption* come about?
- The answer is found in Christ – he writes: 'if due satisfaction be made, none but God *can* make and none but man *ought to* make. So – it is necessary for the *God-man* to make' (*Cur Deus Homo*, II.vi).

Which of these theories do you prefer, and why? If you have time, research what the Scottish Dunce – Duns Scotus (1266–1308) – thought. Far from dim, he has some of the most interesting ideas about incarnation and redemption in Christian tradition.

 Sample Questions

Identification (AO1): What was Pentecost? (1)

Identification and Explanation (AO1): Give two details of the death of Jesus. (2)

Explanation (AO1): Explain two contrasting images / metaphors of redemption. (5)

Evaluation (AO2): 'The Resurrection of Jesus is of supreme importance to Christians.' Evaluate this statement. In your answer you should give developed arguments to support the statement and arguments to support a different point of view. You should refer to Catholic teaching and reach a justified conclusion. (12)

EXCURSUS: conscience and redemption in Catholic Teaching

Redemption and the Human Condition

Saviour? No thanks! It stands to reason if humanity doesn't need saving there is no need for a saviour. There is no need for a redeemer if there is no need for redemption. Many people have held this opinion, and figures such as Marx, Nietzsche and Freud have contended that humanity can perfect itself better if free from religious convictions.

The evidence? Yes please! The wisdom of the Catholic tradition and indeed common experience says the opposite. G. K. Chesterton wittily observed that original sin is the doctrine that has most evidence to support it – even infants grab rattles and bash each other. Humanity needs saving from itself *and it knows it* through *conscience*!

Conscience

Sat nav for the soul: In Catholic teaching, each human being has an inborn moral compass that points towards good rather than bad. Like an inner *voice of God*, conscience acts as *guidance for life. Gaudium et Spes*, 16, says:

'In the depths of his conscience, man detects a law which he does not impose upon himself, but which holds him to obedience. Always summoning him to love good and avoid evil, the voice of conscience when necessary speaks to his heart: do this, shun that.'

As noted in the very first lesson, Catholics should have deep respect for the views and opinions of others and be happy to engage in discussions about human destiny and our role in the world in every context and in every age. This principle is enshrined in the teachings of Vatican II on conscience where, in the document on religious freedom, *Dignitatis Humanae* 3, it says: 'In all their activity a man or woman is bound to follow their conscience in order that they may come to God, the end and purpose of life.'

Individual dignity: Humans know from their conscience that they will be judged – and therefore are in need of redemption. But conscience is not a negative thing – it is the opposite. Just as a parent guides a child through love, conscience is a sign of intimate belonging to God and part of each person's human dignity. The document continues:

'For man has in his heart a law written by God; to obey it is the very dignity of man; according to it he will be judged. Conscience is the most secret core and sanctuary of a man. There he is alone with God, Whose voice echoes in his depths.'

The community call: Yet this does not mean people fly solo through life. In fact, conscience *involves us* with the lives of others and calls us to act in ways that serve the common good:

'In a wonderful manner conscience reveals that law which is fulfilled by love of God and neighbour. In fidelity to conscience, Christians are joined with the rest of men in the search for truth, and for the genuine solution to the numerous problems which arise in the life of individuals from social relationships.'

Informed conscience – the duty to listen: In Catholic understanding, each individual has a duty to *inform* their conscience, to listen to the Gospels and pay heed to Church teaching on matters of faith and morality. However, while people can be mistaken and from ignorance be a bit clueless as to how to act, the warning that the Church gives is that if someone continually 'slings God a deaf 'un' and ignores their conscience, it can lead to them not even seeing what they should do:

'Hence the more right conscience holds sway, the more persons and groups turn aside from blind choice and strive to be guided by the objective norms of morality. Conscience frequently errs from genuine lack of knowledge without losing its dignity. The same cannot be said for a man who cares but little for truth and goodness, or for a conscience which by degrees grows practically sightless as a result of habitual sin.'

Conscience and Redemption

Thus in the Catholic tradition, conscience is part of the *experience* of redemption. Conscience helps believers find their way through life, but by reminding them that 'all have fallen short of the glory of God' it is also a constant reminder of the need for God's mercy made visible by the saving action of Jesus.

Conscience in other Christian Traditions

Protestant Christians: In Protestant traditions, the emphasis upon being 'born again' and a sense of *personal salvation* mean that *individual* conscience may be regarded as even more important than in the Catholic tradition, which emphasises obedience to Church teaching in faith and morals. While this might be thought to weaken the sense of *common* cause, it is not necessarily so. For example, *the Christian Conscience* was the rallying cry among nineteenth-century activists like William Wilberforce (1759–1833) when they campaigned for the end of slavery.

'I felt my heart strangely warmed. I felt I did trust in Christ, Christ alone for salvation, and an assurance was given me that he had taken away my sins, even mine, and saved me from the law of sin and death.'

John Wesley, founder of the Methodists

Extreme Christian Fundamentalists: Among certain extreme Christian groups, the role of conscience may not be treated with the same importance since there can be a tendency to emphasise total obedience to the biblical texts despite what one's conscience might say, even if it means doing things like picking up snakes (see Mark 16:18).

Liberal Christians often follow theories from psychology and sociology and attribute conscience less to the 'voice of God' and more to the internalised 'voice of parents' or of the surrounding culture. For this reason they are sometimes critical of the Christian Church being too involved in moral questions. They claim that it can create a sense of guilt and be burdensome to people rather than liberating. They are inclined to see redemption in terms of renewing a vision of true humanity rather than it involving too great a sense of recompense for human sin.

Liberal Secularists of no religious persuasion take this one step further and can be very suspicious of any restrictions on human action or of heeding any inner voice of reproach. The religious critique of this position is that wherever conscience is repressed and humanist ideologies are imposed, as in the Nazism and Communism of the twentieth century, the consequences have proved genocidal for vast populations worldwide.

Discussion

In a recent book, *Conscience: Rediscovering the Inner Compass*, Robert Solomon from the Methodist tradition quotes an old Tamil saying: 'The guilty heart will be uneasy', and points out that modern lie detectors work on the same principle because our bodies are sensitive to our conscience even if we try and ignore it! Do you agree that the guilty heart is always uneasy? Do you think you could fool a lie detector? And is George Michael correct to suggest in 'Careless Whisper' that guilty feet can't dance properly?

Q Sample Questions

Evaluation (AO2): 'Conscience has no relevance as a guide for Christian life.' Evaluate this statement. In your answer you should give arguments to support the statement and arguments to support a different point of view. You should refer to Catholic teaching and reach a justified conclusion. (12)

Practices - Eucharist and Redemption [AQA Spec 3.1.4.4]

CORE IDEA

In this section the meaning and significance of the Mass as the 'source and summit' of the Christian life will be explored. As part of this, key prayers in the ritual and different understandings about 'sacrifice', 'Real Presence' and 'Eucharistic Adoration' will also be examined.

Redemption and Mass: the source and summit of Christian life

Saving mystery: As noted above, the focus of this unit on redemption is the *mystery of salvation* – sometimes called the *paschal* mystery.

Life and liberation: Just as Israel was miraculously *saved* from slavery and death in Egypt following the sacrifice of a lamb that was then partaken of in a sacred meal, so Catholics believe that it is the sacrifice of Jesus and the partaking of the Eucharist which makes present the miracle of deliverance from the slavery of sin and the power of death.

Real Presence: Catholic understanding of the Mass as a saving meal is not merely symbolic. Catholics believe that the Body of Christ is present in the people gathered by God in love and especially in the sacramental bread and wine transformed in love by God.

Source and summit: For this reason, the Mass is understood as 'the source and summit' of the Christian life. 'Source' because Mass celebrates *redemption*, which is liberation from sin; 'summit' because Mass restores *communion* between God and humanity.

Sunday obligation and holy days: Since the Mass is an expression of what the Church is, Catholics are expected to attend Mass once a week on Sundays, the 'Lord's day', and on other special feast days such as Christmas and All Saints.

To build the Kingdom: The last act of Mass is the *missa* – the sending forth of the people of God to preach the Good News and build His Kingdom on earth.

'For the liturgy, "through which the work of our redemption is accomplished", most of all in the divine sacrifice of the Eucharist, the outstanding means whereby the faithful may express in their lives, and manifest to others, the mystery of Christ and the real nature of the true Church.'

Sacrosanctum Concilium, 2

KEY TERMS

Sacrifice of the Mass =
The Catholic and Orthodox belief that the Mass both commemorates and re-presents the mystery of redemption.

Real Presence =
The Catholic and Orthodox belief that Christ is sacramentally present in the consecrated bread and wine of the Eucharist.

Eucharistic Adoration =
The devotion whereby believers honour Christ present in the Blessed Sacrament.

Words of Institution =
The words of Jesus at the Last Supper offering the bread and wine to the disciples – 'This is my body, this is my blood, do this in memory of me.'

Memory Moment

Mass as Redemption

Once more we can use the shape of the Mass to call to mind the story of redemption. Fill in the blanks ...

i. IN THE NAME OF THE FATHER, SON AND HOLY SPIRIT

_____

ii. THE RITE OF _____:
The believer acknowledges that they have not lived up to being made in God's image.

iii. THE READING FROM THE OLD TESTAMENT

_____

iv. _____:
Listening to the life of the God-Man, Jesus.

v. THE EUCHARISTIC LITURGY: _____

vi. _____: the *Body of Christ* (made up of the believers) receives the immortal *Body of Christ* (really present in the sacrament). The *Bread of Life* restores the faithful to communion, in love, with each other and God.

vii. THE DISMISSAL: _____

Eucharistic controversy

Although communion is meant to be the ultimate sign of unity, there are important differences in Christian understandings and practice of the Eucharist:

Catholic understanding of Real Presence and Words of Institution:

○ **The Last Supper:** It is clear from the earliest descriptions of Christianity that the bread and wine ritual known as the Eucharist was at the heart of the movement (see 1 Corinthians 11:17–34 and Acts 2:42).

○ **Words of Institution:** The mystique of the gatherings was intensified by the repetition of Jesus' words from the Last Supper: 'This is my body – this is my blood – do this in memory of me'. These are known as the 'Words of Institution'.

○ **Real Presence:** Even among the early followers, these words caused controversy (see John 6:52–53 and 1 Corinthians 11:23–26), but there is no doubt that believers understood the risen Jesus to be present among them in the Breaking of the Bread (see Luke 24:34–35).

○ **Not Sarx but Sacramental:** Sarx is Greek for 'flesh'. Real Presence was never understood as 'fleshy' in the crude sense. Instead, Christ was understood to become *sacramentally* present, 'body, soul and divinity', such that the faithful could receive him as he promised under the form of bread and wine.

THE WORDS OF INSTITUTION
'For I received from the Lord what I also passed on to you: The Lord Jesus, on the night he was betrayed, took bread, and when he had given thanks, he broke it and said, "This is my body, which is for you; do this in remembrance of me." In the same way, after supper he took the cup, saying, "This cup is the new covenant in my blood; do this, whenever you drink it, in remembrance of me.'
(St Paul in 1 Corinthians 11:23–25)

Catholic understanding of the *Agnus Dei* and sacrifice

- As noted above, the Last Supper was a celebration of the Passover Lamb, which was the liberation meal of Israel.

- John the Baptist had called Jesus 'the Lamb of God', and the Words of Institution ('This is my body which is [given] for you') also identify Jesus with that role which equals redemption!

- Since ancient times this has been commemorated in the Christian Eucharist by the *Agnus Dei* – the 'Lamb of God' prayer – recited or sung before the faithful received the Communion.

- Catholic Christians therefore see Mass as a re-*presentation* of the sacrifice of Jesus. It makes that *past* moment of grace *present* as a promise of *future* glory.

Non-Catholic Christian contrasts

- **Eastern Orthodox** Christians have a very similar understanding of the centrality of the Eucharist in the practice of their faith. Like Catholics, they believe in the Real Presence of Christ in the Holy Communion and therefore see the Eucharistic sacrifice as essential to the *divinization* of humanity, which is the core of their spirituality.

- **Protestant** Christians place less emphasis upon the Eucharist and are very much against the notion that Christ's one saving sacrifice on Calvary is repeated in any way. They understand Jesus' words at the Last Supper as *symbolic* and reception of the bread and wine primarily as a commemoration *to do this in memory of me* without the sacramental intensity of 'Real Presence'.

- **Anglican** Christians vary in their views. 'High Church' Anglicans celebrate the Eucharist every Sunday and have an understanding of sacrifice and Real Presence which is very close to that of Catholics. Others who are 'Low Church' are more like Protestant Christians. They see the ritual as commemorative rather than sacrificial and celebrate Holy Communion less frequently – perhaps once a month.

- **Non-denominational Fellowships:** Some Christians seek to avoid disputes relating to the Eucharist and emphasise table fellowship rather than liturgy as an act of sharing. They point out that Jesus shared many meals with all sorts of people, and when groups like the 'Full Gospel Businessmen' gather they share a normal meal together followed by an after-dinner exhortation or witness to the Christian life.

🛡 Doctrine Detectives: Eucharist, Friendship & Transubstantiation

St Thomas Aquinas pondered this mystery more than most and connects it together through *friendship.* He pointed out that 'the words of friends when parting' are most significant. For this reason, Jesus *commits* himself to be *really present* in the Eucharist because it *is in the very nature of friends to want to be together.* Yet Jesus also said: 'No greater love hath anyone than to lay down their life for their friends' (John 15:13), and the Eucharist is thus rightly understood as a **sacrificial** moment of love. Exactly how Christ was present in the Eucharist, Thomas Aquinas considered a mystery, but he followed the Lateran Council IV of 1215 in proposing *transubstantiation* as a subtle and revered explanation in the Catholic tradition. Simply put, this meant that the substance of the bread and wine changed but the appearances remained the same. You can check out his poetic version of this theory in the famous hymn *Adoro te devote* – often translated as 'O Godhead hid'.

Eucharistic Adoration

The Real Presence of Christ in the Blessed Sacrament has led to the devotion known as *Eucharistic Adoration.*

A large consecrated Host is placed in a special ornamental artefact called a *monstrance* – from the Latin for 'to show' – and in prayerful fashion, people venerate Christ's presence among them.

Sometimes incense is used to emphasise the holiness of Christ's presence.

Adoration often concludes with *Benediction* – 'the blessing' – when the minister makes the sign of the cross over the people with the monstrance.

> This prayer custom seems to have originated in the Middle Ages and was given great importance when the Pope instituted the feast of Corpus Christi in 1264.
>
> St Thomas Aquinas wrote special hymns for that first celebration which are still used today.
>
> That festival was characterised by public processions to honour Christ present in the sacrament – these still occur today and are a common feature of prayer at Lourdes.

England was renowned for its devotion to the mystery and it led to a whole series of mystery plays being written which helped to teach the people the redemption story. Disagreements about 'Real Presence' led Protestants to discourage the practice, and even today, many Protestants are uncomfortable with the devotion because they think it risks being idolatrous.

Sample Questions

Identification (AO1): Identify two aspects of the Words of Institution. (2)

Explanation (AO1): Explain how 'Real Presence' influences Eucharistic Adoration. Refer to Catholic teaching in your answer. (5)

Evaluation (AO2): 'Christians do not need to celebrate the Eucharist.' Evaluate this statement. In your answer you should give arguments to support the statement and arguments to support a different point of view. You should refer to Catholic teaching and reach a justified conclusion. (12)

Unit 5A Church and the Kingdom of God – Forms of Expression: Drama and the Faith Journey [AQA Spec 3.1.5.1]

CORE IDEA

Catholic understanding of the Church as the pilgrim people of God is explored through the study of enacted prayer, holy journey and religious drama.

The Pilgrim People of God

° This section of our course looks at the Church. When we think of church it is often visual things that first come to mind, like sacred artefacts, arched windows and architecture. However, the Church is much better understood as a pilgrim people of God – a group of people together on a journey through life, growing towards communion with God, in service to one another and to the world.

° 'Pilgrim people of God' captures the idea that far from being a group of smug individuals, the Church is a community on a journey through life but always in need of God's guidance and mercy. A band of the blessed and the broken, a tribe of triumph and trouble, a family of saints and sinners, a people of prayer and penance, yet a people called to serve.

° The idea of Church as the pilgrim people of God is not just something written on a page, it is actually something that is expressed through enacted prayer and holy journeys, and reflected in religious drama.

° In this section we will look at the Stations of the Cross as enacted prayer and at pilgrimage as a holy journey, and use *Les Misérables* as an example of religious drama, all as forms of expression which lead us into a deeper understanding of what the mission of the 'Church' means in vocation and in service.

1st Station of the Cross, Jesus is condemned to death. Stained glass window in St Lawrence Church in Kleinostheim, Germany. Zvonimir Atletic / Shutterstock.com

KEY TERMS

Pilgrim People of God =
A description of the members of the Church.

Stations of the Cross =
A prayer based on the crucifixion of Jesus.

Pilgrimage =
A prayerful journey to a holy place.

Part 1 How the Stations of the Cross reflect Catholic beliefs about the Church as a people of God on a sacred journey of suffering with Christ

a) More than words: Prayer is not just about saying words. In fact, sometimes it may involve no words at all. Just as people who have no voice can communicate using sign language and a kind look can convey comfort to a bereaved friend, and just as Jewish people have prayed by re-enacting the Passover meal every year for millennia, Christians can pray by using movement, gestures or drama. One example of this is the simple act of walking or journeying.

b) Stations of the Cross are a good example. These don't involve trains but they do signal a journey! The *Stations of the Cross* arose as an alternative form of pilgrimage for Christians who were unable to make the journey to Jerusalem, enabling them to walk the *Way of the Cross*, the route followed by Jesus to his crucifixion on Calvary. They can be found on the walls of most Catholic churches.

c) They are a prayerful journey. Catholics pray the Stations of the Cross by walking around the church and pausing to reflect and pray at each picture as they meditate on the scene. In the simple act of walking, they are making an act of prayer, indicating that they wish to accompany Jesus in his suffering.

d) Stations look different but consist of the same 14 scenes. Stations in different Catholic churches are produced by different artists, but all depict 14 scenes from Jesus' journey on Good Friday, from being condemned to death until his body was laid in the tomb. In some churches there is a fifteenth Station representing the Resurrection on Easter Sunday.

e) The Stations are:

1 Jesus is condemned to death

2 Jesus carries his cross

3 Jesus falls for the first time

4 Jesus meets his mother

5 Simon helps Jesus carry his cross

6 Veronica wipes the face of Jesus

7 Jesus falls for the second time

8 Jesus meets the women of Jerusalem

9 Jesus falls for a third time

10 Jesus is stripped of his clothes

11 Jesus is nailed to the cross

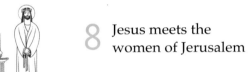

12 Jesus dies on the cross

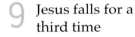

13 Jesus is taken down from the cross

14 Jesus is laid in the tomb

Illustrations / © Roger Smith

Adolfo Pérez Esquivel painted a series of Stations of the Cross in 1992 to mark the 500th anniversary of the arrival of Columbus in the Americas. He depicted Jesus as the Suffering Servant (Isaiah 53), walking to Calvary alongside the suffering people of Latin America. What do these Stations say about the Church's journey of service?

Stations and Servanthood: The Stations call to mind the notion of Jesus as God's suffering servant (Isaiah 52:13–53:12) – this reminds Christians of their call to be servants also.

Take up the Cross: Jesus told his followers they would have to 'take up the cross' (Mark 8:34). This enacted prayer helps Christians to bear their own burdens, and to get up again even when they fall and to unite their sufferings to Jesus (Colossians 1:24).

Part 2 Pilgrimage as a dramatised holy journey and the meaning and significance of pilgrimage to holy sites, including Jerusalem, Rome, Walsingham and Lourdes

a) Pilgrimage is life: Pilgrims leave their familiar surroundings, make new friends, set God as their goal and travel towards their destination. Pilgrimages symbolise *life* as all Christians are travelling on their life journey towards God.

b) Pilgrimage is biblical: This Christian tradition follows in the earlier Jewish tradition of pilgrimage to worship at the Temple in Jerusalem, something Jesus himself did when he was a child (Luke 2:41–42).

c) Pilgrimage is prayer: Since the early days of Christianity, pilgrimage to holy places has been a way for Christians to pray for themselves or for others and to renew their faith.

d) Pilgrimage and penance: Traditionally, pilgrimages have involved hardship – people had to save up their money and make long and difficult journeys. This connects with the idea that they are a form of *penance*, expressing sorrow for failing to live up to God's call.

e) Pilgrimage and reconciliation: Catholics and Orthodox Christians will also often go to the sacrament of confession/reconciliation as a further sign of their sorrow and desire to change.

f) Pilgrimage and transformation: People often testify that a pilgrimage has *changed* them. It is as if being in a different place, being with different people, being in a different routine of prayer and hearing different preaching enables people to have a new sense of God in their lives.

g) Pilgrimage and literature:

On journeys, people have the chance to share their lives and share their memories. One of the most famous books written in English is *The Canterbury Tales* by Geoffrey Chaucer (c.1343–1400), which tells the amusing, racy and holy stories of a group of pilgrims travelling from London to pray at the tomb of St Thomas à Becket in Canterbury. John Bunyan also wrote his famous *Pilgrim's Progress*, which is an allegory of the Christian life recounted as a journey.

Canterbury Tales, Woodcut 1484.

Discussion

When does a journey become a pilgrimage? What journeys in your own life could be seen as pilgrimages?

h) Pilgrimages are different: The grotto in Lourdes, France, became a pilgrimage site in 1858 when news spread that a young girl called Bernadette had seen a vision of Our Lady there. Some people were healed of their illnesses or infirmities after washing in the new spring in the grotto. Sick people still come here for healing of the body, but many more pilgrims visit for healing of the soul.

Basilica of the Immaculate Conception, Lourdes, France.

Pilgrims began to visit Rome after St Peter was martyred there. Eventually, a huge basilica was built over his tomb. People still come to pray at the tomb of the first leader of the Church for his intercession. Often, they also come to seek a blessing from the current leader of the Church, the Pope.

St Peter's Basilica in Rome, Italy.

In fifteenth-century Walsingham, England, a noblewoman named Lady Richeldis reported that she had visited in a vision the home of the Holy Family in Nazareth. Lady Richeldis built a reconstruction of the house she had seen and it became a place of pilgrimage. There are both Anglican and Catholic shrines in Walsingham and, as well as their personal petitions, many people come here to pray for unity.

Priory ruins, Walsingham, England. Richard Croft / geograph.org.uk

Jerusalem is a pilgrimage destination for Jews, Muslims and Christians. For Christians, it is the city where Jesus suffered, died and appeared after his Resurrection. Christian pilgrims seek to grow in understanding and love of Jesus as they experience some of the places he too experienced.

The Dome of the Rock on the Temple Mount in Jerusalem, Israel.

In the 2010 film *The Way* (Cert 12), one man walks the 'Camino', an ancient pilgrimage route through France and Spain ending at the tomb of St James in Santiago de Compostela. Three fellow pilgrims, Sarah, Joost and Jack, discuss whether hardship is a necessary part of pilgrimage. Why might they think this is so? Do you agree? Why/why not?

🛡 Bible Detectives

Journeys feature throughout the Old and New Testaments, and some would say *the whole Bible is the journey of the People of God* – of highs and lows as their understanding grows of how God wants them to be.

Among the most famous are the journeys of the Israelites out of Egypt and through the desert, the journey of Elijah to Mount Horeb, the journey of Tobias with the Archangel Raphael, the journeys of Jesus and the journeys of St Paul around the Mediterranean, to mention but a few.

Can you find where some of these are in the Bible? Did you know that '40' is a number meaning 'transformation' in the Bible? Are there any journeys with '40' in them?

Memory Moment

Station to Station

- With the person next to you, pick a number from 1 to 14 and see if you can remember which 'Station' you would be at!
- If I was going on a mega-pilgrimage to shrines associated with the Holy Family, then with Peter, then with Mary, then with Jesus, would I visit Rome, then Walsingham, then Jerusalem, then Lourdes?

Part 3 Drama and the Christian vocation

Lastly, having looked at prayer as journey and pilgrimage, it is important to explore how Catholic understandings of mission and evangelism are expressed in drama, and to look at the influence of such drama.

Les Misérables, **the famous book, show and film, tells the story of Jean Valjean,** an ex-prisoner who, in a moment of weakness, steals church silver and experiences God's mercy via the wronged priest, who chooses not to accuse him of theft. Building on this experience of mercy, Valjean goes on to become an honest businessman and mayor, in turn showing mercy to his employees and others whom he encounters.

Spoiler alert! When he fails to help one of his employees and she falls on hard times and eventually dies, Valjean raises her orphaned daughter, Cosette. Years later he rescues Cosette's injured beloved from the conflict during the Paris Uprising of 1832. Meanwhile, Valjean is pursued by his one-time prison guard, who shows no mercy and is determined to imprison him again, but who, utterly unable to fathom Valjean, finally commits suicide. In his old age, Valjean sees Cosette in the arms of her beloved and dies peacefully, greeted at death by Cosette's grateful mother.

Alexandre Rotenberg / Shutterstock.com

The drama is full of insights into the Catholic understanding of mission and evangelism. In pardoning Valjean, the priest lives out the mission that all Catholics have – to act with love and mercy towards others – and Valjean experiences this as an encounter with God. It is sometimes said that actions speak louder than words, and as well as talking about it, a committed Catholic will evangelise by living his or her faith. St Francis of Assisi said: 'Preach the Gospel and, if you need to, use words.'

> Watch *Les Misérables*, 2012 (Cert 12) from 8.00 to 13.55. Imagine yourself in Jean Valjean's place. What do you feel when the priest shows you mercy? Why do you think this had such an effect on Valjean's life?

Q Sample Questions

Identification: Give two scenes which form part of the 'Stations of the Cross'. (2)

Connection/comparison (AO1): Explain two ways in which the Church can be understood as the 'pilgrim people of God'. (4)

Evaluation task (AO2): 'Pilgrimage only has meaning if it is to a distant holy place.' Evaluate this statement. In your answer you should give arguments to support the statement and arguments to support a different point of view. You should refer to Christian teaching and reach a justified conclusion. (12)

Extension Exercise: Labyrinths

The labyrinth of Chartres Cathedral.
Photo / Ssolbergj

Prayerfully walking a labyrinth is another ancient form of dramatised journey. A labyrinth is different from a maze – it is not possible to become lost in a labyrinth. Can you work out why? What does this say about the faith journey? Research Chartres Cathedral and find out why its labyrinth was made and in which century.

Discussion

Can you think of any other films, shows or TV programmes that reveal something of the Catholic understanding of mission and evangelism? What influence do you think such dramas have?

Discussion

What signs of the Kingdom do you see around you among family, friends and your wider community?

Beliefs and Teachings about the Kingdom of God [AQA Spec 3.1.5.2]

CORE IDEA

The Kingdom of God is central to the teaching of Jesus. In this section we explore how that can be understood through the Lord's Prayer, through insights from Catholic Social Teaching and through the documents of the great gathering of the Catholic Church known as the Second Vatican Council.

Part 1 Understanding the Kingdom through the Lord's Prayer

a) The Lord's Prayer is one of the most famous treasures of the Christian tradition. It is based on Matthew 6:9–13. When Jesus' disciples asked him how to pray, Jesus taught them the Our Father, also known as the Lord's Prayer. At heart it is a kingdom prayer, since in it Christians pray, 'Thy kingdom come, thy will be done on earth as it is in heaven…'

b) The Kingdom on earth? What Jesus meant exactly by 'the Kingdom' has intrigued saints and scholars for centuries. It seems clear that at first the disciples thought he was challenging the Roman Empire and proclaiming a new Judean kingdom in which they would have the top jobs (Matthew 20:20–28)! While 'King of the Jews' was on Jesus' death warrant (John 19:19), he does not seem to have presented anything like a 'normal' kind of kingdom.

c) The Kingdom in heaven? So is the Kingdom in heaven? The logic of the Lord's Prayer suggests not – if *wherever God's will is done, the Kingdom is present*, then *'on earth as it is in heaven'* implies the task at hand is nothing less than to unite heaven and earth. But how?

d) Jesus' miracles were signs of God's Kingdom. The miracles of Jesus were signs of the Kingdom of God. They showed God's compassion for humanity and the transforming mission of Jesus: to free people from whatever was binding them, be it sickness or death (John 9; Luke 7:11–17), hunger or oppression (Matthew 14:13–21; Mark 5:1–20).

e) Jesus' parables revealed God's Kingdom. To explain the Kingdom, Jesus used parables. For example, the Kingdom is of great value (Parable of the Pearl); it has a slow beginning but will grow to include more and more people. (Parable of the Mustard Seed); it grows secretly without people realising (Parable of the Seeds); it transforms the world (Parable of the Leaven); people will respond in different ways to the invitation to be part of the Kingdom (Parable of the Sower); there are consequences to ignoring or rejecting the invitation (Parable of the Net); yet no one should get ahead of themselves and judge who is part of the Kingdom (Parable of the Weeds).

f) Is the Kingdom for losers? Unlike our world in which riches, fame and power make people most important, Jesus taught that the Kingdom of God is a place where the least important people, such as children, the poor and the outcasts, are the most valued. Indeed, the *Beatitudes* (Matthew 5:1–13) teach that blessedness and happiness are not what we normally think they should be (see Unit 2c).

KEY TERMS

Kingdom of God = The central message of Jesus' preaching.

The Lord's Prayer/ Our Father = The prayer Jesus taught his disciples.

Reconciliation = The act of restoring peace between two parties in conflict with each other.

Sacrament of Reconciliation = Sacrament in which a Catholic confesses sins to a priest and is reconciled to God and the Church.

Catholic Social Teaching = A collection of teachings by Church leaders reflecting on social issues in the light of scripture.

Encyclical = A long letter written by the Pope to the Church and the world.

g) The Kingdom calling of Christians. In heaven, God's will – which is Love – is done perfectly. Here on earth, where things are less than perfect, God's people are called to seek and to live out God's will, thus making the Kingdom present for the benefit of everyone. In this sense, the Kingdom might be better understood as *a grace*, not *a place*; as *a vocation*, not *a location*.

What signs of the Kingdom can you see in this story? Many Catholic parishes have a branch of the St Vincent de Paul Society, which supports local people in need. Youth SVP for 11–14-year-olds and SVP B-Attitude for 14–18-year-olds operate in schools as well as parishes.

'There are not many places where teenagers can meet in a faith environment outside of attending Mass and this is why I love being a member of the Youth SVP … Our group has done many projects over the last year and a half. The one we do most regularly is going to talk to the elderly residents at a local care home. This is my favourite project because all of the people are so welcoming and friendly, and it is very interesting to hear about their lives.'

Liberty Rowe, 14

Part 2 Understanding Catholic Social Teaching on justice, peace and reconciliation as signs of the Kingdom

a) Reconciliation is a sign of the Kingdom and the Church's mission. Jesus taught: 'Blessed are the peace makers, for they will be called children of God' (Matthew 5:9). After his resurrection, Jesus appeared to his disciples and said, 'Peace be with you,' and sent them out with the power to forgive sins (John 20:19–23). Therefore the Church believes that reconciliation, with God and with each other, is at the heart of the Kingdom of God and part of the Church's mission.

b) The Kingdom is a place of justice. The Catholic Church teaches that peace is not possible without justice. A major gathering of bishops known as the Second Vatican Council (see below) taught that 'Peace is not merely the absence of war … Instead, it is rightly and appropriately called an enterprise of justice' (*Gaudium et Spes*, 78).

c) The Church and the poor. The Catholic Church has always recognised that it is not God's will that any human being created in God's image should be treated unjustly. Members of the early Church shared their possessions so that no one should be in need (Acts 2:45), and through the centuries, the great monasteries of Christendom became places of charity and pioneers in agriculture, education and healthcare.

d) Pope Leo XIII. Saints and Church leaders down the ages have left examples of working in charity and for justice. But in 1891, when Pope Leo XIII wrote his encyclical *Rerum Novarum* ('Concerning New Things'), Catholic teaching on social issues of injustice began to be written down. Pope Leo wrote that employers should treat their workers justly, paying a fair wage and giving fair working conditions.

e) Catholic Social Teaching is a sign of the Kingdom. Since Pope Leo XIII, many popes have written Bible-based guidance on the social issues of the day which, together with documents written by bishops, saints and leaders of the Church, have become known as 'Catholic Social Teaching'. They are full of wisdom about how to live in justice and peace, making God's Kingdom more visible in the world.

🛡 Dockyard Detectives

Research the London dock workers' strike of 1889 to find out how the Church got involved and how this may have influenced Catholic Social Teaching. Watch 0:00–4:11 at **https://www.youtube.com/watch?v=P3x3SNiUySc** OR choose one social issue of interest to you (e.g. refugees, conflict or unemployment) and investigate what Catholic Social Teaching has to say about it.

Practical Challenge

Watch this film as an introduction to Catholic Social Teaching: **http://cafod.org.uk/Education/Secondary-schools/Films** Discuss any points that arise.

Memory Moment

The Lord's Prayer is so good, it can help you with your exam!

Our Father who art in heaven – Believers are children of the Heavenly Father.

Hallowed be thy name – God's name is to be honoured as Holy, but this can only happen if,

Thy kingdom come – Establishing the Kingdom of God is central to the mission of Jesus and his disciples and all believers who follow him.

Thy will be done, on earth as it is in heaven – This is what makes the Kingdom come about. Jesus is not talking about a particular place, but a way of life. Earth should become a place of God's love just as heaven is; earth should be a place where the last are treated as well as the first, for we are all made in the image of God.

Give us this day our daily bread – Essentially a plea that our basic needs each day are met, since stockpiling excess is not recommended (see Luke 12:16–21)! Note also, however, that this calls to mind the gift of the manna in the desert (food for the journey [Exodus 16:13–16]) and the gift of the Christian Eucharist (foretaste of the Kingdom [Matthew 26:29]).

And forgive us our trespasses, as we forgive those who trespass against us – This can mean the writing off of money debts or the forgiveness of wrongdoing. Both are pretty difficult but are essential virtues of the Kingdom, according to Matthew 18:21–35. Unless we go some way to living in generous mercy we will never live in the way that God loves.

And lead us not into temptation but deliver us from evil – The word 'temptation' is closer to the notion of being spared from 'a time of trial', which Jesus says is part of living the Kingdom (Matthew 11:11–15). 'Evil' is linked to the Devil, who is the enemy of the reign of God, which is why the exorcisms of Jesus are a sign of the Kingdom.

Part 3 'Vatican II' – The Second Vatican Council, 1962–65. Understanding the hierarchy of the Church and its consultative nature as reflected in Vatican II, the history of the Council, and the four key documents and their themes.

a) Pope John and a new Pentecost: In the rapidly changing world of the 1960s, Pope John XXIII gathered all the bishops of the world together with people of all faiths for a major council in Rome, famously saying: 'Throw open the windows of the Church and let the fresh air of the Spirit blow through!'

b) Two catchphrases summed up the project of the Council. One is French – *ressourcement* – which can be translated as the challenge to go 'back to the roots' of Christianity; and the other is an Italian word, *aggiornamento*, which can be translated as 'up-to-dating'. In this way the Council avoided being either crustily old-fashioned or superficially trendy – it was re-presenting the ancient wisdom of the faith while being sensitive to the 'signs of the times'.

c) A Council for the whole world: The Pope wanted to enable the Church to do God's work and serve the whole people of God on earth. He also hoped the Council would help to bring all Christian Churches together – Vatican II promoted relations of respect and dialogue with people of other faiths.

d) Two popes, three years, four sessions: The four Council sessions lasted over three years, as the hierarchy – the Pope and and the bishops – consulted with laypeople, all guided by the Spirit, to arrive at a common discernment on how God was leading the Church. Pope John XXIII died in 1963. Pope Paul VI was elected and steered the Council to its completion.

e) Four key documents, or Constitutions, were written by the Council, and they slowly but dramatically changed the way the Church worshipped and engaged with the world around it. Each Constitution had a long title as well as a Latin name.

f) Synod of Bishops: After the Second Vatican Council, Pope Paul VI established a Synod of Bishops as a permanent institution to keep alive the spirit of cooperation that had been fostered by Vatican II. The Synod still meets regularly to discuss and discern on Church matters, and most recently met to discuss the family in 2014–15.

Dei Verbum
(Dogmatic Constitution on Divine Revelation)

Themes: The Word of God is communicated through Scripture, Tradition and the teaching authority of the Church (Magisterium), all linked and directed by the Holy Spirit.

Impacts: Before Vatican II, Catholics tended to just hear scripture in church, but were less likely than Protestants to read the Bible as part of their prayer. Vatican II led to groups of lay-people gathering to study scripture together, and reading the Bible became a normal part of life for committed Catholics.

Lumen Gentium
(Dogmatic Constitution on the Church)

Themes: The Church, formed of the whole people of God, is the sacrament of salvation. The Pope and the bishops are there to serve the people. Every member of the Church is called to participate in the Church's mission.

Impacts: Before Vatican II, Catholics could have the impression that the task of preaching the Gospel and serving the Kingdom was only down to priests or nuns. After this document, the Church emphasised more clearly that it was the vocation of everyone to take part in the mission of the Church in the service of the world.

Sacrosanctum Concilium
(Constitution on the Sacred Liturgy)

Themes: The Church proclaims the Gospel not only in word but also in sacrament, or by sacred signs. The people of God in their entirety are to be involved in this worship, so these signs must be intelligible.

Impacts: Before Vatican II, Mass everywhere was in Latin and everyone, including the priest, faced the same way, emphasising the act of sacrifice. This document was a prompt for the liturgy to be translated into the language of each country so that everyone could understand what was being said. The altar was moved so that the priest faced the congregation, so that in turn the symbolic actions of sacrifice and of sacred banquet could be more visible.

Gaudium et Spes
(Pastoral Constitution on the Church in the Modern World)

Themes: The Church must read the signs of the times and interpret them in the light of the Gospel. The Church is part of the world and proclaims the Gospel by its service to the whole human family, helping to make humanity's history more human.

Impacts: Before Vatican II, there was perhaps a sense that the Church should primarily keep apart from the world. While it is right and proper for the Church to be distinct, this document made it clearer that in order to serve the Kingdom, the Church had to be involved in social issues. Catholic agencies such as CAFOD grew in awareness of their responsibility not only to respond to suffering but to address its causes.

An official portrait of Pope Paul VI by BastienM.

1965 'The joys and the hopes, the griefs and the anxieties of the men of this age, especially those who are poor or in any way afflicted, these are the joys and hopes, the griefs and anxieties of the followers of Christ.'

Gaudium et Spes, 1

Pope Francis by MikeDotta / Shutterstock.com

2013 '... Today we have to say "thou shalt not" to an economy of exclusion and inequality. Such an economy kills. How can it be that it is not a news item when an elderly homeless person dies of exposure, but it is news when the stock market loses two points? This is a case of exclusion. Can we continue to stand by when food is thrown away while people are starving? This is a case of inequality.'

Pope Francis, *Evangelii Gaudium*, 53

Sample Questions

Identification (AO1): What was the Second Vatican Council? A gathering of Jewish leaders / A gathering of councillors / A gathering of Church leaders / A gathering of the European Union. (1)

Explanation (AO1): Explain two ways in which the Lord's Prayer influences beliefs about the Kingdom of God. (4)

Evaluation (AO2): 'The government should pay more attention to Catholic Social Teaching.' Evaluate this statement. In your answer you should give arguments to support the statement and arguments to support a different point of view. You should refer to Christian teaching and reach a justified conclusion. (12)

Sources of Authority

[AQA Spec 3.1.5.3]

CORE IDEA

In this unit students will explore the meaning and significance of Mary as model of discipleship in the Church and understand why her Magnificat is a controversial Kingdom prayer. Students will then learn of the 'Marks of the Church' as One, Holy, Catholic and Apostolic, and of how these lead to a better understanding of the Magisterium.

Part 1 Scripture

Detail from Mother of God of Kyhos by Simon Ushakov

KEY TERMS

Magnificat = The Song of Mary from Luke 1:46–55.

Four Marks of the Church = One, Holy, Catholic, Apostolic.

Magisterium = Teaching authority of the Catholic Church.

Infallible = 'Indisputable' pronouncements made by a pope in the name of the Church.

Pontifical = To do with the Pope (or 'pontiff').

Conciliar = To do with the great Church councils of bishops.

The Magnificat – Mary's Song of Praise

And Mary said,
'My soul magnifies the Lord,
and my spirit rejoices in God my Saviour,
for he has looked with favour on the lowliness of his servant.
Surely, from now on all generations will call me blessed;
for the Mighty One has done great things for me,
and holy is his name.
His mercy is for those who fear him
from generation to generation.
He has shown strength with his arm;
he has scattered the proud in the thoughts of their hearts.
He has brought down the powerful from their thrones,
and lifted up the lowly;
he has filled the hungry with good things,
and sent the rich away empty.
He has helped his servant Israel,
in remembrance of his mercy,
according to the promise he made to our ancestors,
to Abraham and to his descendants for ever.' (NRSV)

a) Mary – a disciple's faith: Mary was clearly a girl of some faith who is challenged by the Angel to believe that God will bring about something miraculous in her. In saying *'Let it be done'* she is an example to the Christian challenged to believe that the power of God is greater than human wisdom.

b) Mary – a disciple's courage: Mary is sometimes thought of as timid because when asked if she would bear God's Son she promised to be the 'maidservant' of the Lord (Luke 1:38). Yet she had to have tremendous courage to accept this challenge. In those days, to be pregnant but unmarried was potentially fatal, and it can be noted that Mary has the presence of mind to leave town immediately and go to visit her cousin Elizabeth in the hills (Luke 1:39).

c) Mary – a disciple of the Kingdom: Elizabeth's greeting, 'Hail Mary', has come down through the generations as a prayer, but less well known is Mary's response. Her song of praise in Luke 1:46–55 is known by its Latin name: 'Magnificat' which translates the Greek word *megalunei* - 'mega-praise'! In it she strongly proclaims 'Kingdom/first-shall-be-last' themes that will later be found on the lips of Jesus as the proud are scattered, the powerful dethroned, the hungry fed and the rich sent away empty (verses 51–53).

d) Mary – disciple and mother: The *Catechism of the Catholic Church*, 2619 describes the Magnificat as the song of both the Mother of God and the Church which characterises the generous offering of Mary's whole being in faith (2619 and 2622).

e) Mary – disciple first and last: Mary was present at Jesus' first miracle at Cana (John 2:1–12), she was one of the few disciples who did not desert him at the cross (John 19:25), and she waited with the disciples in the upper room for the coming of the Holy Spirit at Pentecost (Acts 1:14). Therefore the Catholic Church sees Mary as a model for all Christian disciples (see *Lumen Gentium*, 52–65).

🛡 **Doctrine Detectives**

Did you know that public recitation of the Magnificat has been banned at certain times in certain countries? For example, after Argentinian mothers whose children had disappeared in the Dirty War (Guerra Sucia) placed the words of the Magnificat in the main square, the military outlawed any public display of Mary's song. Why do you think this was the case? Where else have people tried to silence Mary? Which famous non-Christian leader recited this banned prayer when his country won independence?

Part 2 **The Four Marks of the Church**

Pentecost

If Mary is the model for disciples, how are the whole group of disciples and followers of Jesus supposed to 'hang together'? Catholics believe that just as Mary's 'yes' to the Spirit gave birth to Jesus, so the 'yes' of the disciples to the Spirit at Pentecost gave birth to the Church as:

The New-born by Georges de la Tour, 1640

One – the action of the Spirit is to form the believers into One mind and heart as the Body of Christ (see Acts 2:44 and 4:32);

Holy – although believers are imperfect, in the Spirit the very holiness of God is poured out upon the Church (Acts 2:17);

Catholic – this literally means 'according to all' or 'universal'. At Pentecost, despite all the differences that existed in race and language, the Spirit revealed through the gift of tongues that the Good News was *universal* – for all nations (Acts 2:4–11);

Apostolic – at Pentecost, beginning with Jesus' chosen twelve apostles, the whole Church is sent out to proclaim the Good News to all (Acts 2:32 and 37–42).

Creed

These Four Marks thus became part of the Nicene Creed as the Church grew in its understanding that it was:

One = called to unity as one in the Body of Christ;

Holy = called to be Holy, set apart for a special purpose by God;

Catholic = called to be 'Universal' that the faith be proclaimed to all;

Apostolic = called to remain rooted in the living tradition of the apostles of Jesus.

Apostolic

It may seem odd, but for Catholics, this fourth Mark is perhaps the most important. Why?

Leadership: St Peter was chosen from among the twelve apostles and given leadership of the Church by Jesus (Matthew 16:18). Peter eventually became leader of the Christians in Rome, which was effectively the capital city of the world at the time of the Roman Empire.

The successors of Peter who led the Church in Rome continued in that overall leadership role, and when there were disputes among local bishops, they made appeal to Rome for judgement. The 'Pope' is the name given to the Bishops of Rome who through this tradition are considered to be the leaders of the whole Catholic Church.

Teaching: This 'teaching' role of the Bishop of Rome became key to Catholic understanding of the Church. It helped to safeguard unity *one-ness*; it was a reminder that the Church was founded by God, not man – *holy*; and it emphasised the Church was *catholic* – bearing one *universal* message for *all*.

Authority: Lastly, it emphasised the Church as *apostolic*. As the first apostles visited early Church communities to support them, they chose leaders from among the communities and laid their hands on them, as a sign of passing on the authority that the apostles had received from Jesus (see Acts 15:22–33). These were the first bishops. In the Catholic tradition, people can't just self-declare themselves as Christian leaders. Rather, it is through this **'apostolic succession'** of one bishop handing on authority to another down through the centuries that the Church has retained cohesion.

Part 3   Magisterium

The idea of *apostolic succession* leads directly to an understanding of Magisterium – the teaching authority of the Church.

The Pope and the bishops in any given age are known as the 'Magisterium' of the Church. Catholics believe that by following the guidance of the Magisterium, they are following the guidance of Jesus, from whom the bishops received their authority. It works in two ways – conciliar and papal.

Conciliar Magisterium: When a doctrine is pronounced, it is normally done with great solemnity as the result of a Church Council – a gathering of bishops called by the Pope, the Bishop of Rome. For example, the Council of Trent, 1545–63, pronounced that Christ is 'really, truly and substantially present' in the consecrated bread and wine of the Eucharist. Most of the traditional doctrines of the Church and the great creeds have been authorised by such Councils.

'The joys and the hopes, the griefs and the anxieties of the men of this age, especially those who are poor or in any way afflicted, these are the joys and hopes, the griefs and anxieties of the followers of Christ. Indeed, nothing genuinely human fails to raise an echo in their hearts. For theirs is a community composed of men. United in Christ, they are led by the Holy Spirit in their journey to the Kingdom of their Father and they have welcomed the news of salvation which is meant for every man. That is why this community realises that it is truly linked with mankind and its history by the deepest of bonds.'

Gaudium et Spes, 1

Likewise:

Synods are like a mini-council which is convened by the Pope to look at a specific issue – for example, in 2015 there was a Synod on family life.

The Pope and Magisterium: As noted above, the Pope has had a long-standing teaching role, and exercises 'ordinary' Magisterium in his teaching and his encouragement of the faithful by means of his preaching, his special letters called 'encyclicals' and other communications.

St Peter's Basilica in the Vatican, Saint Peter's Square, Rome, Italy. IR Stone / Shutterstock.com

The Pope and infallibility: This is much misunderstood and does not mean the Pope knows what lottery numbers are going to win or can declare it to be raining when it is sunny! It is rooted in the promise of Jesus to Peter that 'whatever you bind and loose on earth shall be bound and loosed in heaven' (Matthew 16:19). The Church teaches that in consultation with worldwide bishops and the people of God, the Pope can make infallible pronouncements on matters of Christian faith and morals. For example, in 1950, when Pope Pius XII defined the dogma of the Assumption of Mary – that Mary was taken up to heaven body and soul – both the bishops and the ordinary faithful were consulted and the eventual pronouncement simply clarified a strong tradition which the Church had affirmed for centuries.

Conciliar *and* Papal Magisterium: It cannot be emphasised enough that the Pope and the bishops endeavour to work together. For example, the bishops at the Second Vatican Council (1962–65) gave a new emphasis to Catholic Social Teaching in *Gaudium et Spes* 'Joy and Hope', 1, which popes since then have followed up (e.g. Pope Francis in *Evangelii Gaudium* 'The Gospel of Joy', 53–54). This change of emphasis has led to intense engagement with numerous global institutions and a sustained critique of worldwide injustice through Catholic Social Teaching.

Point of comparison: Protestant Churches do not place the same importance on apostolic succession. Because they believe so strongly in the absolute authority of scripture, many of them are uneasy that the Pope or the bishops should have teaching authority, still less *infallibility*. They may agree with many of the doctrines of the Catholic Church but regard many traditions, including devotion to Mary, as non-biblical and therefore wrong.

Memory Moment

It may be helpful to use 'discipleship' as the way to link the elements of this unit.

> **MARY – MODEL DISCIPLE**
> Through faith, courage and Kingdom proclamation in the Magnificat, Mary models discipleship and gives birth to the body of Christ.

> **APOSTLES AT PENTECOST**
> Mary is present with the apostles at Pentecost – the birthday of the Church as the new body of Christ.

> **MAGISTERIUM**
> Peter as Bishop of Rome retains focus on unity and teaching, helping believers grow as disciples modelled on Mary.

> **APOSTOLIC CHURCH**
> One, Holy, Catholic and Apostolic. Apostles hand on teaching authority to successor bishops united under 'Peter'.

Ⓠ Sample Questions

Identification (AO1): In the Gospels, which of the following is NOT said of Mary mother of Jesus? She was engaged to a man named Joseph / she believed the message of the Angel / she visited her cousin Elizabeth / she gave birth to Jesus in a palace. (1)

Explanation (AO1): Give two reasons why the Magnificat is a Kingdom prayer.

Evaluation task (AO2): 'Magisterium is essential for the unity of the Church.' Evaluate this statement. In your answer you should give arguments to support the statement and arguments to support a different point of view. You should refer to Catholic teaching and reach a justified conclusion. (12)

Practices – the Church as the Body of Christ [AQA Spec 3.1.5.4]

CORE IDEA

How the Kingdom command to love our neighbour in concrete ways is expressed in the work of Catholic agencies, in the specific vocations of individuals and in the life of one important Catholic figure.

Part 1 Church in action 1

The Church as the Body of Christ. In 1 Corinthians 12:24 St Paul wrote, 'God has so arranged the body … that there may be no dissension within the body but that the members may have the same care for one another.' Members of the Church are called to care for others, and this has led to many Catholic organisations which express neighbourly love in concrete ways.

DePaul UK was set up by Cardinal Basil Hume in 1989 and is named after St Vincent de Paul, the patron saint of charity. Its work includes measures to help young people avoid becoming homeless, as well as practical help for people who have ended up on the streets. DePaul UK supported more than 3,000 young people in 2015.

For example, Daniel fell out with his family and began taking legal highs, which became addictive. When he lost his flat because he could not afford the rent, he ended up sleeping rough on the streets, begging and shoplifting.

Daniel applied to DePaul UK for a room at Simonside House, the charity's base in Newcastle which has 13 bedrooms and 24-hour staffing. Daniel moved in and now is receiving help to stop his addiction and is in contact again with his family. He says, 'Since moving here I haven't looked back. Things have been a lot better.'

Go to DePaul UK's website to find out more: **uk.depaulcharity.org**

CAFOD (Catholic Agency for Overseas Development) was started in 1960 by a group of Catholic mothers who encouraged parishes to fast one Friday in Lent and give the money towards a mother and baby clinic in Dominica. Their efforts were so successful that the bishops set up CAFOD as the official aid agency for Catholics in England and Wales. Today CAFOD campaigns and raises awareness within England and Wales and fundraises to support partners tackling poverty and injustice in more than 30 countries.

KEY TERMS

Vocation = From the Latin for 'calling'.

Laity/Laypeople = From the Greek for 'people' – the baptised people of God, members of the Body of Christ.

Martyrdom = Literally 'to give witness' but now usually associated with giving one's life for a cause.

Consecrated life = Religious people living in community who take vows of poverty, chastity and obedience.

Holy Orders = The sacrament received by men ordained as deacons, priests or bishops.

For example, one CAFOD partner is the Sisters of St Clare on the outskirts of El Salvador's capital city, San Salvador. Gangs have divided the area where the sisters live and work. There are often shootings. Young people who have to cross gang - borders in order to reach school are afraid to attend. With few other prospects, many young people are drawn into gang life.

Photo / CAFOD

With support from the sisters, young leaders plan and run a Saturday project for younger children. Isabel (15) is a leader. She says: 'The course is about gathering a group of young people together and teaching us to pass our knowledge on to the next generation, children from, say, five to nine years old. We will work with them so that when they get to our age they'll say to themselves, "Let's change things in our country!"'

Go to CAFOD's website to find out more: **cafod.org.uk**

 **Church Detectives**

Find out about a Catholic agency that works in your local area. How would you produce a leaflet that encourages people to support it or volunteer for it?

Part 2 Church in action 2

Vocation – love at the heart: Pope John Paul II said: 'Love is the fundamental and innate vocation of every human being' (*Familiaris Consortio*, 11). St Paul agrees – he says that if you even perform miracles without love, you're a nobody (1 Corinthians 13:2).

Vocation – Kingdom at heart: It has been mentioned before that the Kingdom of God is better understood as a vocation rather than a location, as part of Jesus' call to 'live life to the full' (John 10:10). Catholics believe that every person has a unique contribution to make as a member of the body of Christ, whether it be spectacular or secret, whether obvious or hidden (see 1 Corinthians 12).

Vocation – state of life: Each Catholic finds and lives his or her own unique vocation, whether it be through ordained ministry, consecrated life or as a layperson, married or single.

Laypeople: Most Catholics live their vocation as laypeople, either single or married. Single Catholics serve God in the world in many and varied ways, supported by the Catholic community. Many are active in Church groups such as Life or the SVP and others have roles in Eucharistic ministry, sacramental preparation, missionary volunteering or as part of specialist chaplaincy provision. Others may simply honour God more generally by living honest and kind lives according to scripture – for example, the Golden Rule of Jesus: 'In everything do unto others as you would have them do to you' (Matthew 7:12), and Micah: 'acting justly, loving tenderly and walking humbly with God' (Micah 6:8).

'God has created me to do Him some definite service. He has committed some work to me which He has not committed to another. I have my mission. I may never know it in this life, but I shall be told it in the next.'

Part of a prayer by
Blessed John Henry Newman

Married people are called to model the love of Christ and his Church in a special way through the sacrament of matrimony (see Ephesians 5:25–33). As 'the domestic Church' they have a life-giving role within the home since family love can be an especial grace for brothers and sisters, grandparents, cousins, uncles and aunts. '*Ubi caritas, Deus ibi est*' – Where there is love, there is God.

Consecrated life: Religious sisters and brothers dedicate themselves to God and to their religious community. They normally do so by taking Kingdom vows of poverty, chastity and obedience which confront the three great worldly idols of riches, lust and power. This sets them free from worldly ambition to serve God wholeheartedly by living, praying and working in the community. Strictly speaking, 'nuns' and 'monks' are those religious such as the Poor Clares and the Carthusians who take the same vows but remain 'enclosed' within convents and monasteries to serve God's people by spending their whole lives praying for the people of the world.

Lucernarium Easter Vigil. Photo / Fr Lawrence Lew OP

Catholic Sisters.

Ordained ministry: Some Catholics feel called to Holy Orders, which, in the Catholic tradition, means becoming a deacon, priest or bishop. Because Christ was male, as were the apostles, the Catholic Church and the Orthodox Church teach that only men can be ordained. While bishops are appointed by and are obedient to the Pope, deacons and priests live their vocation by making a promise of obedience to their local bishop to go wherever he says to meet the needs of the Church. Normally based in a parish, they follow the command of Jesus (Matthew 28:19–20) by celebrating the sacraments for the people and helping people grow in faith and discipleship. Others may have more specialist ministries – for example, in hospitals or in youth work. Most priests are single and celibate as a sign of giving their whole lives for the sake of the Kingdom (Matthew 19:12), but deacons and priests who have come from other denominations may be married with families (1 Corinthians 9:5).

> The Call of the Kingdom: 'Do not worry . . . Seek first the Kingdom of God and all things shall be given unto you.'
>
> Matthew 6:33

Point of contrast: Many Protestant Christian denominations do not recognise these different states of life and have a much looser sense of organisation or 'hierarchy'. It can be argued that the letter of Peter supports this in saying that all Christians form 'a chosen race, a royal priesthood, a holy nation, God's own people' (1 Peter 2:9). This looser sense of organisation and authority does bring with it the risk of fragmentation. Since the Reformation in Europe in 1517, thousands of Protestant Churches have come into existence, which runs counter to the prayer of Jesus – 'may they all be one' – and runs counter to the 'Four Marks of the Church' which are part of the Nicene Creed that has for centuries defined Christian belief.

Part 3 Church in action 3

a) Catholic practices of justice, peace and reconciliation are vividly expressed in the life of Oscar Romero.

b) Archbishop Oscar Romero of El Salvador was shot dead while saying Mass on 24 March 1980. At the time, his country was governed by the

Statue of Oscar Romero from façade of Westminster Abbey, London. hakne1 / Shutterstock.com

wealthy, who were oppressing the poorest people with help from the army. Thousands were imprisoned, tortured or murdered, or simply disappeared.

c) Romero denounced the violence in his Sunday sermons, which were broadcast by radio, and called for peace and justice for the poorest. He became known as 'the voice of the voiceless'. CAFOD, supported by Catholics from Britain, funded the rebuilding of his radio station when it was bombed by those who did not want his voice to be heard.

d) Romero knew his life was under threat but continued to speak out. A few days before he died he ordered the army to stop killing people: 'In the name of God, and in the name of this suffering people whose cries rise to heaven more loudly each day, I beg you, I implore you, I order you, in the name of God, stop the repression!'

e) Romero was a martyr. After Romero's death, many of the ordinary people of El Salvador began calling him 'San (Saint) Romero' and came to his tomb to pray. In 2015, Pope Francis declared that Romero was a martyr and he became known as 'Blessed Oscar Romero', or 'beatified' – the first step to being officially declared a saint.

Memory Moment

Watch the five-minute film, *Oscar Romero: A Life for God and the Poor*, at: cafod.org.uk/ Secondary-schools/Romero

Which event helped Romero to discern that his vocation was to serve the poorest people? What inspires you most about Romero's life?

How does the Catholic faith of people like Oscar Romero and Sean Devereux affect their actions? What can their example teach us about reconciliation in other parts of the world today, or between individuals?

Sean Devereux

Sean Devereux taught PE at a school in Surrey run by the Salesians – a community founded by St John Bosco to work with young people. After two years of teaching, Sean departed for Liberia to do missionary work with the Salesians. When a civil war began, the school

www.seandevereux.org.uk

where Sean was teaching was forced to close and Sean moved into aid work, often putting himself in danger to defend the rights of others. He once said, 'While my heart beats, I have to do what I think I can do, and that is to help those who are less fortunate.' In 1993, at the age of 28, while organising relief for starving people in Somalia, Sean was shot and killed by a lone gunman.

 Sample Questions

Identification (AO1): Give an example of a Catholic agency which lives out the call to 'love your neighbour'. (1)

Explanation (AO1): Explain two ways in which a vocation to the priesthood or religious life shows Kingdom values. Refer to Christian teachings in your answer.

Evaluation (AO2): 'Serving the Kingdom should not Involve Martyrdom.' Evaluate this statement. In your answer you should give arguments to support the statement and arguments to support a different point of view. You should refer to Catholic teaching and reach a justified conclusion. (12)

Christian Life, Death and Eternity – Forms of Expression: Artefacts and Eschatology [AQA Spec 3.1.6.1]

CORE IDEA

In this section, the Paschal candle will be analysed as a symbol of resurrection, and the religious significance of Christian burial and memorial traditions will be examined.

Part 1 The Paschal candle: symbol of Christ's resurrection

It may be a surprise, but 'officially' the greatest feast of the Christian year is not Christmas, it is Easter, because it celebrates the promise of eternal life through the resurrection of Christ.

In a series of three special ceremonies, the Last Supper is commemorated (on Holy Thursday), followed by the Crucifixion (on Good Friday) and the Resurrection (on Easter Night). Together, this *triduum* captures the *Paschal*, or Passover, mystery which has been spoken of before – a sacred meal, a sacrificial death and liberation from slavery to new life.

As night falls on Holy Saturday, the Easter Vigil begins and the first action of the priest is to prepare and then light the Easter or 'Paschal' candle. This is the prime symbol of the resurrection of Jesus, and the congregation are then led in procession singing 'Christ our Light'.

The church is in darkness and each member of the congregation takes a candle which is lit from the Easter light, forming a river of light as they take their places.

The people then remain standing while a song of resurrection joy, such as the ancient *Exultet*, is sung.

The Paschal candle has many features which are full of symbolism:

- The **flame** first symbolises the *light of Christ* which has come into the world and which 'darkness could not overpower' (John 1:4–5).

- The **candle** contains a high proportion of beeswax because it is a *precious* artefact representing Christ. Bees even get a mention in the *Exultet*.

- **Alpha and Omega** are the first and last letters of the Greek alphabet and symbolise Christ understood as 'the first and last, the beginning and the end' of all things, of life, death and creation (Revelation 22:13).

- **The Cross** is the symbol of Christ's death, which is remembered on Good Friday as the saving action of love by which 'Christ our Passover, has been sacrificed *for us*' (1 Corinthians 5:7).

KEY TERMS

Paschal candle = The Easter symbol of Christ's resurrection in Catholic churches.

Eschatology = Literally, the study of 'last things'.

Paschal candle.
Photo / Fr Lawrence Lew OP

- **Anno Domini – 'the Year of the Lord'** – is always written on the candle to remind the faithful that Jesus is Lord of time, 'the same yesterday, today and forever' (Hebrews 13:8).

- **Five wounds** – five spiked studs each containing a grain of incense are inserted into the candle as the priest concludes the consecration of the candle, saying: 'By his holy and glorious wounds, may Christ our Lord guard us and keep us, Amen.'

- **Big is beautiful** – the Paschal candle is traditionally by far the biggest candle in the church – normally around three feet high, though in the Middle Ages, the *Sarum Rite* for Salisbury Cathedral directed it should be 12 yards high! These massive candles were often then melted down and made into little tapers for use at the funerals of the poor.

- **Pedestal** – on Easter night the candle is used to bless the waters of baptism and is placed on a special high pedestal at the front of the church, casting the hope of everlasting life over all the people. For this reason it is lit throughout the seven weeks of the Easter season and at every baptism and funeral.

Part 2 Christian memorial artefacts

Christian belief in life after death can also be seen in the design of memorials, tombs and remembrance gardens.

Catacombs: In the earliest days of Christianity, the underground burial places of the believers were called 'catacombs', which consisted of long tunnels with burial slots, or *loculi* ('little places'), cut into the walls, which were then sealed.

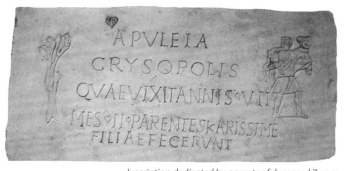

The Catacombs of San Gennaro Gonzalo, Naples, Italy. Sanchez / Shutterstock.com

Christ the Good Shepherd: Sometimes the seals were made of cut stone which could be decorated. The one shown here commemorates a seven-year-old girl who has passed. She is entrusted to the care of the Good Shepherd (see John 10:1–18), who lays down his life in order to take it up again. The sheep who belong to him listen to his voice and he will lead them home.

Inscription dedicated by parents of deceased 7-year-old girl, Apuleia Crysopolis; Good Shepherd and bush found in the Catacomb of St Callisto, Rome, Italy.

As Christianity became more accepted and Christians became more prosperous, decorative tombs or *sarcophagi* became more common. The one shown here has Christ the Good Shepherd in the centre but also depicts another sign of belonging – 'I am the vine, you are the branches' (John 15:5) – and believers partaking of the fruit of that vine which is eternal life.

Churchyards and cemeteries: As the centuries unfolded, Christian burial traditions became more public; indeed,

Detail from an early Christian sarcophagus on the site of a Christian chapel in Ostia Antica, the ancient port of Rome. Photo / Fr Lawrence Lew OP

older churches, abbeys and minsters can seem surrounded by death! There are tombs outside and inside, and sometimes there are graves under slabs in the aisles.

Although this might seem spooky, it makes sense in terms of Christian belief that there is ONE communion of saints – those alive on earth and those alive in God. Eventually, large graveyards or *cemeteries* for the vast numbers of Christian faithful became the norm.

The land for these was always consecrated and there are strict rules even today about any building or redevelopment of burial sites. While funeral vaults are more common on the continent, in the UK, burial in the ground is most common and simple headstones act as memorials of people's lives. These often carry a prayer of dedication and a message of affection from the family which fit very well with the Christian virtues of faith, hope and love (1 Corinthians 13:13).

Part 3   Cremation and memorial gardens

- For a long time cremation was rare among Christians and was even banned as a practice in the Catholic Church between 1886 and 1966. In religious terms, burial better imitates what Christ underwent, it seems more scriptural, and in some ways fits more with the imagination of the dead rising to new life (see 1 Thessalonians 4:13–18). Nowadays, the Catholic Church 'permits cremation, provided that it does not demonstrate a denial of faith in the resurrection of the body' (CCC 2301).

- There are numerous reasons why Christians prefer it; some are to do with the practicalities of cost and others to do with space and the possibility cremation allows for people to bury the ashes of their loved ones, regardless of where they may have died, in a single family plot. Very common nowadays among Christians is the practice of interring ashes in simple memorial gardens, which seem more attractive to some.

- Natural burial grounds: an even more recent phenomenon which some Christians choose is interment in a natural burial ground, where the emphasis is more on being one with Creation than it is in the traditional graveyard. Marked by very simple plaques, the plots are usually unconsecrated and tend to lack Christian symbolism – the planting of a shrub or rose bush near or on the burial plot is more common.

🛡 Design Detectives

As well as the Good Shepherd, a popular image of Jesus in the catacombs was as Jonah and the whale – why do you think that was? It took several centuries for the cross/crucifix to become a common symbol of hope in Christian burial grounds, and yet now it is probably the most common. What are the possible reasons for this? Do John 3:14–15, Numbers 21:4–9 or 1 Corinthians 1:18–25 shed any light on the reasons?

Jonah Cast Forth By the Whale, by Gustave Doré (d. 1883).

RIP- suggests the person will rise again after death showing catholic beliefs. unlike cremation you can't resurrect.

Memory Moment

Without looking at the picture of one, draw a Paschal candle with all the key elements. Then annotate the drawing with explanations of their symbolic meaning.

Q Sample Questions

Identification (AO1): When is the Paschal candle first lit? Christmas/Pentecost/Easter/Ascension. (1)

Comparison (AO1): Describe two features of the Paschal candle and explain their meaning. (4)

Evaluation (AO2): 'The meaning and significance of Christian burial memorials is confusing.' Evaluate this statement, giving arguments to support the statement and arguments from a different point of view. You must refer to Catholic teaching and reach a justified conclusion. (12)

Unit 6B

Life and Death in Beliefs and Teachings [AQA Spec 3.1.6.2]

CORE IDEA

In this section on Catholic beliefs about the afterlife, concepts such as death, judgement, heaven, hell and purgatory will be examined and compared with other Christian views.

Part 1 Paul and early Christian belief

- Christian beliefs about the afterlife are rooted in the Easter shock, the bodily Resurrection of Jesus.

- St Paul, writing within twenty years of the events described in the Gospels, is aware of the mind-boggling nature of the event. He was called a parrot or babbler for talking about it, but while some mocked him, others were intrigued (Acts 17:18 and 32).

- Paul, though, is convinced of the truth of the event. He met the risen Jesus and spent the rest of his life proclaiming its truth (Acts 9:3–6, Galatians 1:11–12).

- Facing questions from the Church in Corinth as to how the dead can be raised, Paul is driven to compare the way a grain or seed 'dies' when it is planted and how miraculous it seems when the wheat grows. He continues:

- 'What is sown in weakness, is raised in power, a physical body is raised as a spiritual body ... just as humanity has borne the image of the man of dust Adam so it will also bear the image of the man of heaven Jesus' (1 Corinthians 15:42 and 49).

- In other words, we are stuck with an image of ourselves that is rooted in our limited mortal physicality, which is like looking in a tarnished mirror. The risen human being will be like the risen Lord, beyond imagination but not beyond faith, hope and love (1 Corinthians 13:12–13).

- St Paul believes this truth is a source of great consolation to Christians, who should not mourn as those do who have no hope: 'Death where is your victory?' he writes, 'Death where is your sting?' (1 Corinthians 15:55).

Part 2 Particular judgement: heaven, hell and purgatory

Another question Paul faced was what happens to those people who die before the end of time (see 1 Thessalonians 4:13–18). Fast forward 2,000 years, and in a two-sentence sermon, a priest recently gave a discombobulating answer: 'There is a common view going round these days that when we die, we are all going to the same place. Well we are. The judgement seat of God.' And then he sat down!

KEY TERMS

Four Last Things = A traditional Catholic shorthand for 'death, judgement, heaven and hell'.

Death = The end of a human being's earthly life.

Heaven = A place of eternal happiness in communion with God.

Hell = A place of eternal unhappiness removed from the presence of God.

Purgatory = A place of preparation for eternal communion with God.

Well, although he might have softened his tone a little, he was perfectly correct to remind his listeners of Christian belief in *particular judgement* – namely, that when a person dies, they are held accountable for their deeds. However, this judgement is imagined (e.g. some people who have had near-death experiences speak of their whole lives passing before their eyes), and Catholic teaching proposes three outcomes:

- The first is that the individual is found worthy to enter into the divine blessing of heaven, united with the saints in the all-encompassing love of God.

- The second is that in the mystery of this moment, although the individual has a longing to be with God, he or she still needs to be freed or 'purged' from some attachment which is holding them back. This state is called 'purgatory'.

- The third is that the individual is found to be utterly attached to rebellion and hatred for God and so is effectively incapable of participating in the divine life.

While Catholic belief in purgatory is controversial for some, it is rooted in the biblical tradition of praying for the dead (2 Maccabees 12:39–45), the idea that purification may be necessary to enter the presence of God (1 Corinthians 3:11–15), and the long tradition of praying for the dead which is evidenced from the catacombs onwards. This only makes sense if at least some among those who have passed can be blessed by such prayers and their fate is not automatically sealed.

Particular judgement of the individual is distinguished from *Final Judgement*, which was connected with the Second Coming of Christ as the cosmic Son of Man and Lord of all. This has formed part of Christian belief from the beginning but again is something that is difficult to imagine, so maybe we need a little artistic help!

All who die in God's grace, but still imperfectly purified, are indeed assured of their eternal salvation; but after death they undergo purification, so as to achieve the holiness necessary to enter the joy of heaven.

Catechism 1030

Memory Moment

Michelangelo's *Final Judgement* and the Four Last Things

Just as Michelangelo contemplated the beginning of all things in the Sistine Chapel, so he imagined the *eschata* – 'the last things'. The four last things in Christian tradition are 'death, judgement, heaven and hell', and this mural paints a powerful picture which is designed to stay in your mind!

Death: All human beings, rich and poor alike, are mortal and so will one day die. Michelangelo emphasises this by the sheer number of figures on the fresco.

Judgement: In this painting we see the central figure of Christ in his second coming as judge of the world. The 'righteous are to his right', but even Mary his mother looks a little terrified as he gestures damnation to those on his left (see Matthew 25:46).

Final Judgement (and the Four Last Things) by Michelangelo.

Heaven and Hell: Below centre in Michelangelo's painting, the angels blow their trumpets to summon the dead (see 1 Thessalonians 4:16). While St Michael reads from the Book of Life, another reads from a much larger Book of Death and the righteous are gathered upwards towards heaven while devils grapple with their harvest of the damned (Daniel 12:2). Note that while the saints bear evidence of their worldly suffering (e.g. St Bartholomew carries his skin, having been flayed alive), the damned are scarcely able to behold their torment, one fellow peeking through his fingers at his fate. In religious terms this serves to emphasise the fact that true torment is being apart from God, rather than the suffering of hardships or difficulties.

Different Christian beliefs about life after death

Although Michelangelo literally paints what has become a classic picture of Christian understanding of the last things, there are inevitably contrasting views because of the speculative nature of what happens after death.

Death: Although traditional Christian belief holds fast to the notion of *bodily* resurrection and the cosmic reconciliation of all things in earth and heaven, many less traditional Christians think that death is the permanent separation of body and soul and that only the soul lives on. They even point to ghosts and near-death experiences of people who 'leave their body' as a form of evidence.

Final Judgement: Liberal Christians are less inclined than traditional Christians to believe in a final judgement or second coming. They point out that the early Christians were mistaken on this and that the fate of an individual is sealed at the moment of death rather than at some <u>future cosmic judgement</u>. Fundamentalist Christians would say the opposite, some groups even claiming that on the Last Day only 144,000 will be taken into heaven.

a few people believe people are judged at eternity the end of the world to see if they are going to heaven or hell.

Particular Judgement: Within Christianity, one obvious difference in belief is that Protestant Christians tend not to believe in purgatory whereas Catholics do. Hence the tradition of praying for the dead is much stronger among Catholics, who will often ask priests 'to offer Mass' for deceased members of their families.

Heaven and Hell: Liberal Christians doubt that an all-merciful God would abandon anyone to eternal damnation. Interestingly, although Michelangelo and others were keen to depict their enemies as being in hell, the Catholic Church has never pronounced that any individual is actually there. On the other hand, it has pronounced that certain people have reached the sanctity of heaven (i.e. the canonized saints).

Bereavement and Consolation: Despite differences in emphasis, the core Christian belief in an afterlife is a deep source of consolation for those who mourn the departed. Maybe Paul should have the last word: 'Death where is your victory, death where is your sting?' The resurrection of Jesus is a sign that sin is forgiven and so humanity can rejoice in the promise of immortality in union with God (1 Corinthians 15:55).

Near-death Experiences: Some Christians set great store by the astonishing testimonies of people such as George Ritchie and Eben Alexander who have had what are called 'near-death experiences'. While even the famous philosopher A. J. Ayer had his atheism shaken by such an event, a wide variety of beliefs emerge from such experiences, not all of which reflect mainstream Christian thinking.

Reincarnation: This is not at all traditional within Christianity nor within the monotheism of Judaism and Islam, but has its strongest associations with eastern religions such as Hinduism and Buddhism.

✡ Doctrine Detectives: Nearly Dead or Nearly Born?

Christianity offers no neat map or satnav for the understanding of afterlife. That said, it does repeatedly use the metaphor of *new life*, so maybe instead of talking to the nearly dead, we should be talking to the newly born, as this popular 'thought experiment' of Hungarian origin suggests:

Two twins were talking in the womb:
Tell me, do you believe in life after birth?

Of course. After birth comes life. Perhaps we are here to prepare for what comes after birth.

Forget it! After birth there is nothing! From there, no one has returned! And besides, what would it look like?

I do not know exactly, but I feel that there are lights everywhere … Perhaps we walk on our own feet, and eat with our mouth.

This is utterly stupid! Walking isn't possible! And how can we eat with that ridiculous mouth? Can't you see the umbilical cord? And for that matter, think about it for a second: life after birth isn't possible because the cord is too short.

Yes, but I think there is definitely something, just in a different way than what we call life.

You're stupid. Birth is the end of life and that's it.

Look, I do not know exactly what will happen, but Mother will help us…

The Mother? Do you believe in the Mother?! Don't be ridiculous! Have you seen the Mother anywhere? Has anyone seen her at all?

No, but she is all around us. We live within her. And certainly, it is thanks to her that we exist.

Well, now leave me alone with this stupidity, right? I'll believe in Mother when I see her.

You cannot see her, but if you're quiet, you can hear her song, you can feel her love. If you're quiet, you can feel her caress and you will feel her protective hands.

Attributed to Útmutató a Léleknek, translated by Miranda Linda Weisz

Which twin are you? Are there any biblical passages you can find that connect with this meditation? Maybe start with John 3. What about 12:24 from the same Gospel? How does St Paul refer to himself (Galatians 1:15, 1 Corinthians 15:8)?

Ⓠ Sample Questions

Identification (AO1): Which of the following is NOT a Christian belief regarding the afterlife: Judgement/ Reincarnation/ Heaven/ Hell. (1)

Explain (AO1): Explain two Christian beliefs about life after death. Refer to (St Paul's) teaching in your answer. (5)

 pg119 ←

Evaluation (AO2): 'Michelangelo's Last Judgement is a misleading expression of Christian belief about the afterlife.' Evaluate this statement giving arguments to support the statement and arguments from a different point of view. You must refer to Catholic teaching and reach a justified conclusion. (12)

Life and Death in Sources of Authority [AQA Spec 3.1.6.3]

CORE IDEA

In this section the aim is to deepen knowledge of the Christian understanding of the afterlife through insights from Scripture (Luke 16), Tradition (Mother Julian of Norwich) and Magisterium (Second Vatican Council).

Part 1 Scripture: the Rich Man and Lazarus

- In Luke 16:19-31 Jesus seems to offer a worked example of what Christians call *particular judgement.*

- A rich man is robed in purple and he dines lavishly – signs of wealth and greed, respectively.

- Worse, though, he flashes the cash, he is *mean* and he does nothing to help the poor man who begs by his gate who is suffering with illness. *This is serious – even the dogs are more kind than he is.*

- Yet death and judgement come to all, and for these two men, *their fortunes are reversed.* The poor man finds himself 'in the bosom of Abraham', but the rich man is in Hades, the place of torment.

- The rich man cries out for help but is told that there is a chasm between them that can't be crossed. *This symbolises the chasm that existed between his table and the poor man at the gate.*

- At last thinking about more than just himself, the rich man asks that his brothers be warned, but this puts him in even more trouble. *Abraham reminds him that Moses and the prophets have long proclaimed the message of God that the rich should take care of the poor.*

- His last throw of the dice: if someone rose from the dead they would listen, he claims. No they wouldn't, replies Abraham. *Even the resurrection of Jesus will not cure some people of selfishness.*

- Last but not least, then as now, it was the rich who were famous and the poor who were forgotten. *In this story, however, the poor man is named – but what was the rich one called? Loser?*

Meaning and significance: the final whistle

- A cynic once remarked that the only things that are certain in life are death and taxes. While rich people especially try to avoid both, death, ultimately, is the great equaliser.

- Some people argue that it is only death that gives meaning to life. Albert Camus said that 'life is the sum of all your choices'. Effectively, what you believe is what your life is, and this parable is a stark reminder that in the Christian tradition there is a final whistle. Made in the image of God, our challenge is to grow more and more in the image of God's Son.

KEY TERMS

Mother Julian of Norwich = A Christian mystic from the Middle Ages.

Lumen Gentium = Literally, 'light of the nations' – an important document on the Church from the Second Vatican Council.

- Now, whether it is classed as a parable or a moral tale, this story has the classic hallmarks of Jesus' Kingdom preaching. There is role reversal, the unexpected happens, and the last ends up first.

- It is a reminder to stay awake, for no one knows the day or the hour when they will be called to account (Matthew 25:13). Most of all, it connects perfectly with the call for humanity to recognise the image of God in the least of our brothers and sisters or face the judgement that is due (Matthew 25:43).

The Rich Man and Lazarus

19There was a rich man who was dressed in purple and fine linen and who feasted sumptuously every day. 20And at his gate lay a poor man named Lazarus, covered with sores, 21who longed to satisfy his hunger with what fell from the rich man's table; even the dogs would come and lick his sores. 22The poor man died and was carried away by the angels to be with Abraham. The rich man also died and was buried. 23In Hades, where he was being tormented, he looked up and saw Abraham far away with Lazarus by his side. 24He called out, 'Father Abraham, have mercy on me, and send Lazarus to dip the tip of his finger in water and cool my tongue; for I am in agony in these flames.' 25But Abraham said, 'Child, remember that during your lifetime you received your good things, and Lazarus in like manner evil things; but now he is comforted here, and you are in agony. 26Besides all this, between you and us a great chasm has been fixed, so that those who might want to pass from here to you cannot do so, and no one can cross from there to us.' 27He said, 'Then, father, I beg you to send him to my father's house – 28for I have five brothers – that he may warn them, so that they will not also come into this place of torment.' 29Abraham replied, 'They have Moses and the prophets; they should listen to them.' 30He said, 'No, father Abraham; but if someone goes to them from the dead, they will repent.' 31He said to him, 'If they do not listen to Moses and the prophets, neither will they be convinced even if someone rises from the dead.'

Part 2   Tradition: the revelations of divine love

In 1395, the *Revelations of Divine Love* was the first book published by a woman in the English language, and for 600 years it has remained a best-seller. Why?

It was written at a tragic time in history. A terrible plague known as the Black Death had raged across Europe, decimating families, villages and entire regions and leaving behind a grief-stricken continent.

On 13 May 1373, from the depths of this dark sadness, struck with illness and waiting for death, a thirty-year-old woman was given in prayer a series of '16 Shewings' or 'revelations' which proved to be of enduring consolation to those that heard of them.

Her insights were a poetic expression of the biblical truth that God's love can transform all things. Whether it be the greatest wickedness or the greatest sadness, the Christian has the certain hope that at the end of time *all shall be well* – indeed, *all manner of things shall be well*.

'Deeds are done which appear so evil to us and people suffer such terrible evils that it does not seem as though any good will ever come of them; and we consider this, sorrowing and grieving over it so that we cannot find peace in the blessed contemplation of God as we should do; and this is why: our reasoning powers are so blind now, so humble and so simple, that we cannot know the high, marvellous wisdom, the might and the goodness of the Holy

Trinity. And this is what he means where he says, "You shall see for yourself that all manner of things shall be well", as if he said, "Pay attention to this now, faithfully and confidently, and at the end of time you will truly see it in the fullness of joy."'

Revelations of Divine Love

It is not known whether she was a religious or layperson at the time of her visions, yet she eventually become famous as Mother Julian of Norwich – a name she was given by the townsfolk since she lived out her days in a prayer cell set into the walls of the Church of St Julian in that city.

Her work is important in terms of Christian eschatology because in poetic and beautiful imagery she confirms the religious message of the Gospels and the powerful words of St Paul in Romans 8:31 and 38–9: 'I consider that our present sufferings are not worth comparing with the glory that will be revealed in us ... for neither life nor death nor anything else in creation will be able to separate us from the love of God that is in Christ Jesus our Lord.'

Among her visions, Julian of Norwich saw the world held like a hazelnut in the palm of the Creator's hand. 'And I saw three things – first that God made it, second that God loves it and third that God preserves it.'

Part 3   Magisterium: afterlife, communion and the future of creation

Although each individual faces death alone, the Church also teaches that believers together form a sacred unity. This 'communion of saints' is unbroken by human mortality; the curtain of death, like the veil of the Temple, is torn in two and the saints in earth and heaven are as one.

But this is not just a message that is of relevance to Catholics or Christians, it is a message for all humanity. Echoing the teaching of St Paul and Mother Julian, it is only in the *fullness of time* that the Church envisages the restoration of *all things*. The Second Vatican Council document on the Church called *Lumen Gentium* – 'Light of the Nations' – says:

'The Church, to which we are all called in Christ Jesus, and in which we acquire sanctity through the grace of God, will attain its full perfection only in the glory of heaven, when there will come the time of the restoration of all things. At that time the human race as well as the entire world, which is intimately related to man and attains to its end through him, will be perfectly re-established in Christ.'

Lumen Gentium, 48

Consistent with this vision of a renewed humanity, consistent with being the light for all peoples, the Church prays for 'all who seek God with a sincere heart' and teaches that all can be saved:

'God predestines no one to go to hell; for this, a wilful turning away from God (a mortal sin) is necessary, and persistence in it until the end. In the Eucharistic liturgy and in the daily prayers of her faithful, the Church implores the mercy of God, who does not want "any to perish, but all to come to repentance": Father, accept this offering from your whole family. Grant us your peace in this life, save us from final damnation, and count us among those you have chosen.'

Catechism of the Catholic Church 1037, cf. *Youcat* #152–162

Memory Moment

These three different insights into the Last Things each have calling and consolation at their heart, which may help you to remember them:

- Consolation in the Call of the Kingdom – the Rich Man and Lazarus – the call for humanity to be generous, for in the end the last shall be first and the suffering consoled.
- Consolation in the Call of the Creator – Revelation of Divine Love – the call for humanity to be at peace, for in the end 'all shall be well'.
- Consolation in the Call of the Church – Vatican II/'Light of the Nations' – the call for all to seek God, for in the end all humanity will be restored in Christ.

🛡 Doctrine Detectives – Argument for the Sake of Heaven!

Three possible discussions:

Though the mind is somewhat boggled by the huge scope of such beliefs, the Church is proposing that all the yearnings of the human heart are ultimately religious desires which are only satisfied in God's eternal love. As St Augustine says: 'Our hearts are restless until they rest in thee.' Do you agree, or can purely human ambitions and achievements be a source of ultimate satisfaction?

Second issue: What is heaven like? Is there any chance of a game of footy? Perhaps most importantly, will there be chocolate? My mother-in-law has never missed Mass on a Sunday but she loves shopping too. She is past 80 now and so recently asked a bishop if there was a Marks and Spencer in heaven. 'All shall be there that is necessary for your happiness,' came the reply. Nailed it. For once, she was lost for words. But do you agree with him? You might want to check out what St Paul says after his visit (2 Corinthians 12:2) and what the Bible says about the *Messianic Banquet* – Isaiah 25:6; Psalm 23:5; Matthew 8:11–12, 22:1–14; Luke 14:15–24; and Revelation 19:6–9. What is the ultimate celebration likened to? Why? Are there any connections with Genesis 3?

Third issue: If Christianity is correct, hope you like singing. Revelation 9:6 suggests the songs of the saints will be like the sound of thundering waters. While the thought of heaven as a mudless Glastonbury might not float your boat, it has inspired some great music and songs down the years. The '*Hallelujah Chorus*' by Handel is one end of the spectrum, but for a ramshackle view of what heaven might sound like, check out 'This Train is Bound for Glory' by Edward Sharpe & The Magnetic Zeros, Mumford & Sons and the Old Crow Medicine Show.

 ## Sample Questions

Identification (AO1): Which of the following sayings is associated with Mother Julian of Norwich? All shall be well/All shall not be well/Well, well, well/Well I never. (1)

Explanation (AO1): Explain two ways in which the Parable of the Rich Man and Lazarus influences Christian understanding of the afterlife. (4)

Evaluation (AO2): 'The Bible is all that Catholics need as a proof that there is life after death.' Evaluate this statement, giving arguments to support the statement and arguments from a different point of view. You must refer to Catholic teaching and reach a justified conclusion. (12)

Life and Death – Practices [AQA Spec 3.1.6.4]

CORE IDEA

This section will explore the way in which Catholic beliefs influence the Sacrament of the Sick, the Care of the Dying and the Funeral Rite.

The Last Rites and Anointing of the Sick

Catholic Christianity has a long tradition of sacramental care for the dying known as 'the Last Rites'. Traditionally, three sacraments are involved – penance, communion and anointing, all of which are seen in the life of Jesus:

- Penance – the *reconciliation* of the individual to God by confession and absolution of their sins as preparation for judgement.

- Communion – the partaking of the bread of life and cup of salvation as *viaticum* – 'food for the journey' through death to life with God.

- Anointing – with the sacred oil for the sick, both as a sign of *healing* from distress and as preparation for death.

Of these three elements, the anointing is regarded as the essential sacrament, and since it includes within the ritual a prayer for the forgiveness of sins, it can only be administered by a priest.

Extreme unction – because of its association with the Last Rites, the sacrament of anointing was known for a long time as *extreme unction* – literally, last anointing. In recent times this has changed greatly and it is much more common for it to be administered as a sacrament of healing for those who are not near to death but who are unwell in mind or body.

To sum up, the Last Rites are a sacramental expression of reconciliation, healing and hope.

The Funeral Rite

The prayers and actions of the funeral rituals are directly influenced by Catholic beliefs about life after death. They are rarely giddy or frivolous but, rather, tend to have a solemn strength about them that can be a source of deep consolation to those who mourn.

Preparation: Once a person has died, the body will be prepared for burial by a professional undertaker who will embalm and dress the body and place it in a wooden coffin. Great care is taken with this as a sign of Christian belief in the dignity of the individual and the sacred nature of both the body and the soul.

The wake or vigil: The body will normally be kept at the undertaker's Chapel of Rest until it is taken to church. Some Catholics, however,

wake - body brought to family house to pray around.

KEY TERMS

Anointing of the Sick = The sacrament administered by the Catholic Church to those who are either unwell or in need of healing.

Last Rites = The sacraments which are often received just before death: confession, communion and anointing of the sick.

will prefer to have the body make its last journey from home, and invite visitors to express their condolences there – this is sometimes called a 'wake'. Still others have the body received into church the night before to keep vigil. Any or all of these allow the mourners opportunities for prayer and consolation.

The funeral: The ritual can take place either on its own or during a celebration of Eucharist, when it is commonly called a *Requiem Mass*.

Procession: The coffin is brought in and placed close to the sanctuary of the church near to the Paschal candle. Upon it are placed key symbols of Catholic belief:

- *The Book of the Gospels* – the Word of God, symbolising faith in Jesus.

- *The Cross* – symbolising the redemption of humanity by his sorrowful death.

- *The Paschal candle* – symbolising the joy and hope of the resurrection.

- *Baptism* – it is also recommended that a white covering cloth be used to symbolise baptism, but in the UK this is normally recalled simply by the sprinkling of the coffin with holy water at the beginning of the ceremony.

- *Incense* – the priest or deacon will often venerate the coffin with a thurible containing burning charcoal and incense, symbolising the sanctity of the body and as a sign of prayer rising to God.

Readings and homily: After a short penitential rite, there are then Bible readings which the family may have helped to choose. There is always a Gospel passage, normally with a resurrection theme – e.g. 'I am the resurrection and the life', 'Do not let your hearts be troubled, there are many rooms in my Father's house.' The rite then requires that the priest or deacon conducting the funeral preach a sermon on the theme of Christian hope in the face of death.

At Requiem Mass, the liturgy of the Eucharist then follows. The Church teaches that although this is not *essential*, it is very fitting for a funeral because it is a sacramental experience of the mysteries of redemption. The life, death and resurrection of Jesus are recalled in prayer, and Holy Communion is understood as a foretaste of the Banquet of Heaven.

Eulogy: If the deceased is not well known to the minister it is common for a member of the family to deliver a *eulogy*. This literally means 'good words' which recall the life of the one who has passed, but it is not *essential* to the ritual, and where this tradition takes place in the liturgy varies from parish to parish.

Prayer of commendation: The prayer of commendation is the last part of the funeral rite whereby the minister and the faithful implore the saints and angels to gather the departed loved one into the happiness of heaven 'where Lazarus is poor no more'.

Committal: The body is then taken either to the graveyard or to the crematorium. The minister will again sprinkle the coffin with holy water as a reminder of the immortality promised in baptism, but this phase of the ceremony calls to mind the mortality of humankind – the fact that even the believer must return to dust in the hope of resurrection.

There are explicit prayers of consolation for the mourners that they will one day be reunited, 'when every tear will be wiped away', and the Lord's Prayer/Our Father is said.

After the final blessing, the crematorium ceremony ends with the slow closing of the curtains. At the graveside, mourners normally sprinkle dust upon the coffin as a sign of mortality, but they may also sprinkle holy water as a sign of immortality and lay flowers as a sign of affection and the promise of new life.

Memory Moment

You may recall that some of the first consoling images in the Christian catacombs were of Christ the Good Shepherd. It should be no surprise, then, that Psalm 23, 'The Lord is My Shepherd', is one of the most common songs/prayers heard at Christian funerals. Although the version given here is in old-fashioned language, by some simple associations it might help you remember the essential components of the Catholic funeral rite.

PSALM 23	THE FUNERAL RITE
The Lord is my shepherd – I shall not want. He makes me down to lie	Death marks the end of human needs – 'Our hearts are restless until they rest in you.' The body is prepared and laid out in the coffin.
In pastures green, he leadeth me the quiet waters by	The body is received into the sanctuary of God and blessed with the baptismal waters.
My soul he doth restore again and me to walk doth make	It is adorned with symbols of restoration and redemption – the Cross and the Paschal candle.
Within the paths of righteousness for his own name's sake	The Bible readings teach the righteous path to those called in God's name.
Though I walk in the valley of shadows and death – I fear no ill	The Gospel proclaimed – darkness, fear and death are scattered by the light of the Risen Christ.
You are there with your rod and staff to comfort me still	Authorised by Christ's Church, the minister encourages the faithful with words of hope.
My table he has prepared in the sight of my foes	At Requiem Mass, the banquet of Eucharist is laid as a foretaste of the promised heavenly banquet.
My head he doth with oil anoint and my cup overflows	All Christians are anointed at Baptism in preparation for the overflowing joy of eternity.
Goodness and mercy all my life will surely follow me	The Eulogy – uplifting stories of the person's life may be retold.
And in God's house for evermore my dwelling place will be	The final commendation that the one being mourned will be gathered into the heavenly place.

Doctrine Debate: care of the dying, sanctity of life and euthanasia

○ Care of the dying is something especially important in Catholic practice.

○ In large part this is due to two fundamental ideas mentioned at the start of the course – that each individual is made in the image of God, and that life is sacred ('the sanctity of life').

○ Christian commitment to care of the dying is evidenced in sacramental practice whereby chaplains and Eucharistic ministers take Holy Communion to the dying and priests administer the Last Rites.

○ It is also clearly evidenced by the hospice movement, which is a feature of UK healthcare today. A hospice is a place where those entering their last weeks on earth are given expert 'palliative' ('pain-relieving') care. Many of them, such as St Gemma's in Leeds, were founded by Christian groups or churches.

St Gemma Galgani.

○ To the modern western mind, 'the sanctity of life' is a radical belief since it means that you belong to God before you belong to yourself! (Yikes!)

○ In turn, this makes sense of the whole biblical testimony which proposes that for humanity to truly flourish, it must listen to the commands of God, not just do what everyone else thinks is right.

- Crucially, the life of Jesus, God's own Son, teaches that innocent suffering is part of life. The challenge of the Kingdom is to go through it rather than go around it (Matthew 16:24).

- For these reasons, Catholics are opposed to *euthanasia*. This term comes from the Greek and means 'good' or 'happy' death, but in the modern day it has come to mean the deliberate termination of a human life by medical means.

- Euthanasia is allowed in some countries but it remains illegal in the UK. Those in favour of it regularly bring 'assisted dying' proposals before Parliament in order to change the law.

- In the recent past these have been opposed by a coalition of religious groups of all faiths who, while sensitive to the suffering of individuals, feel that any change in the law will lead society down a 'slippery slope' such that people who are ill or old – nans and grandads – will begin to feel obliged to opt for euthanasia so as not to be a burden.

- The following table is a simplified summary of the different situations people find themselves in and Catholic responses to secular arguments. You might want to find out the history of a hospice local to you and what its approach to assisted dying is. St Gemma's views can be found on its website: **http://www.st-gemma.co.uk/**

Situation	Secular Argument	Catholic Response
Someone is on life-support machinery.	Those in a deep coma or UWS – 'unresponsive wakefulness syndrome' – should have life support switched off.	Though the Church urges that basic needs should be met, discontinuing of 'extraordinary means' is permitted (see *Catechism* 2278).
Someone is terminally ill.	People should be able to avoid the pain of a drawn-out death and be given fatal drugs instead.	All efforts should be made to ease pain (palliative care), but assisted suicide contradicts the sanctity of life, and remission can happen.
Someone feels life is not worth living.	People should have the choice to die if they want to and to get help from their doctor to do so.	Many of those who survive a suicide attempt regret the attempt. People should be given reasons to live, not to die. Doctors should not have to make such decisions.
Someone is old and weak.	The quality of life of many old people is poor, and they use up healthcare resources and housing. Assisted dying should be an option for all.	Humans are made in the image of God; their value is not based on what they do but on what they are. The old should not be made to feel a burden – after all, they have previously looked after us.

Q Sample Questions

Identification (AO1): What is the Anointing of the Sick? (1)

Explanation (AO1): Explain two ways in which Catholic beliefs about life after death influence how their funeral rites are celebrated. (4)

Evaluation (AO2): 'The Resurrection means Christians should support euthanasia, not oppose it.' Evaluate this statement, giving arguments to support the statement and arguments from a different point of view. You must refer to Catholic teaching and reach a justified conclusion. (12)

Glossary

Abortion = The deliberate ending of a life in the womb.

Abraham = Founding father of Judaism.

Adalat = God is Just.

Adonai = Lord.

Adoptionism = Jesus wasn't divine.

Adultery = A sexual relationship involving a person already married to someone else.

Aetiology = Ancient parables which offer reflections on why things are as they are.

Afikoman = A piece of *Matzah* put aside during the *Seder* meal.

Agapé = Self-giving love.

Akhirah = Afterlife.

Al Chet = General confession.

Alenu = The closing prayer of Jewish services.

Allah = God.

Altar = The central focus of the Christian church – a table-like plinth made of stone or wood.

Amidah = Prayers that are said when standing.

Annulment = A Church declaration that a marriage was not valid.

Anointing of the Sick = The sacrament administered by the Catholic Church to those who are either unwell or in need of healing.

Aron Ha-Kodesh = Ark.

Ascension = Jesus' return to the Heavenly Father.

Āyah = A verse in the Qur'ān.

Azrā'īl = The Angel of Death.

Baptism = The sacramental water ritual of Christian initiation.

Bar = Son.

Bar/Bat Mitzvah = Son/Daughter of the law.

Bat = Daughter.

Barabbas = A violent Judean insurgent, prisoner of the Romans.

Bartimaeus = The blind man Jesus cured at Jericho.

Bat Chayil = Daughter of life.

Beatitudes = The Kingdom blessings of Matthew 5.

Beneficence = The kindness of God.

Beth Din = Jewish court of law.

Bimah = Reading platform.

Blasphemy = Saying or doing something that dishonours God.

Brit = Covenant.

Bullying = Unjustified intimidating behaviour.

CAFOD (The Catholic Agency for Overseas Development) = An international Catholic organisation dedicated to helping the poor.

Canaan = The land between the Mediterranean and west of the Jordan river. In the Bible it is also used as the name for the Promised Land.

Canon = Another word for Bible – the inspired collection of writings sacred to Christians.

Cantor = Leader of prayer usually through music.

Caesarea Philippi = A town in northern Israel.

Capitalism = An economic and political system in which a country's trade and industry are controlled by private owners for profit, rather than by the state.

Catholic Social Teaching = A collection of teachings by Church leaders reflecting on social issues in the light of scripture.

Celibacy = Not being married and not engaging in sexual activity.

Challah = One special plaited loaf.

Challot = Special plaited loaves.

Chametz = Leaven.

Chastity = The virtue of loving people in the right way at the right time.

Chi-Rho & Alpha/Omega = Greek monograms for Jesus.

Christ = Literally, 'anointed one' in Greek.

Christogram = A set of letters signifying Christ.

Chumash = A printed book with daily Torah and synagogue readings.

Chuppah = Bridal canopy.

Circumcision = The removal of the foreskin of a penis.

Cohabiting family = Non-married couple who may or may not have children.

Common good = Policies and actions which benefit everyone, not just particular groups.

Communism = A theory or system of social organisation in which all property is owned by the community and each person contributes and receives according to their ability and needs.

Complementarity = The way in which man and woman have been created to bring out the best in each other.

Conciliar = To do with the great Church councils of bishops.

Covenant = A sacred agreement between God and His people.

Conscience = The inner moral compass of human beings.

Conscientious objector = Someone who refuses to do military service on grounds of religious belief or personal conviction.

Consecrated life = Religious people living in community who take vows of poverty, chastity and obedience.

Contraception = The deliberate use of means to prevent pregnancy resulting from intercourse.

Contraceptives = Means by which sexual intercourse is rendered infertile.

Creed = A statement of belief. The word 'creed' comes from the Latin word *credo*, which means 'I believe'.

Crucifix = A cross upon which the figure of the suffering Jesus has been placed.

Crucifixion = A method of capital punishment by nailing or binding to a cross.

Death = The end of a human being's earthly life.

Dhul Hijjah = The month of pilgrimage.

Dignity = Humans are worthy of respect.

Dignitatis Humanae = The declaration on *Religious Freedom* from Vatican Council II.

Discrimination = Negative behaviour or actions towards an individual or group based on prejudice.

Divine Word = Jesus is God's love spoken in a human life.

Divorce = The legal separation of a married couple.

Docetism = The belief that Jesus wasn't human.

Economic Trinity = God's outermost expression – how God has revealed Godself in human history.

Ecumenical Council = A gathering of all the bishops of the world with the Pope.

El Rachum = God is Mercy (see Deuteronomy 4:31).

Elijah = A prophet of God.

Elul = The sixth month of the Jewish year.

Encyclical = A long letter written by the Pope to the Church and the world.

Ephesians = A letter written by St Paul to a community of Christians in the Early Church.

Eros = Erotic/Sexual love.

Eschatology = The study of 'last things'.

Etz Chaim = The tree of life.

Eucharist = The Christian service, ceremony, or sacrament commemorating the Last Supper, in which bread and wine are consecrated and consumed.

Eucharistic Adoration = The devotion whereby believers honour Christ present in the Blessed Sacrament.

Evangelii Gaudium = 'The Joy of the Gospel' – a letter written by Pope Francis to all Catholics.

Exile = To be forcibly removed from your own country.

Exodus = The second book of the Torah. It means 'The Going Out'.

Extended family = A family which extends beyond the nuclear family to include grandparents and other relatives.

Fairness = God is just.

Familiaris Consortio = A letter written by Pope St John Paul II to Christians today.

Fast = To go without food and drink for a certain period of time.

Force = The morally justified use of violence.

Forgiveness = Letting go of the wrong done to you.

Four Last Things = A traditional Catholic shorthand for 'death, judgement, heaven and hell'.

Four Marks of the Church = One, Holy, Catholic, Apostolic.

Free will = Humans can decide their own actions.

Gan Eden = A place of the dead in paradise.

Gaudium et Spes = Vatican Council II's declaration on *The Church in the Modern World*.

Gemara = A rabbinical commentary on the Mishnah, forming the second part of the Talmud.

Genesis = First book of the Torah in the Hebrew Bible.

Genesis 'Beginnings' = The 1st Book of the Bible.

Genizah = A special storage room in a synagogue for old Torah scrolls and ritual objects which cannot be used any more.

Gethsemane = The place Jesus prayed before his trial.

Glory = The term *doxa* in Greek and *kabod* in Hebrew refers to the inexpressible majesty of God.

God as Benevolent = Creation is God-loved.

God as Transcendent = 'Unrestricted' God is beyond our reality.

Grace = The free gift of God's love.

Gehenna = A place of the dead in punishment (Hell).

Genocide = The intentional killing of large groups of people.

Hādīth = The words and actions of the Prophet Muhammad.

Haftarah = A reading from the Prophets.

Haggadah = A book containing the order of service for the *Seder* meal.

Hajj = Pilgrimage to Makkah.

Halakhah = Observance of the Commandments – literally 'a way of walking'.

Halakhic life = Walking with God.

Hashem = The name of God.

Hashophet = God is Judge (see Judges 11:27).

Havdalah = Separation ceremony made at the end of Shabbat which divides Shabbat from the ordinary working week.

Heaven = A place of eternal happiness in communion with God.

Hell = A place of eternal unhappiness removed from the presence of God.

Heresy = Mistaken belief.

Hesed = God's loving kindness (see Exodus 34:6).

Holy Orders = The sacrament received by men ordained as deacons, priests or bishops.

Holy War = A war waged for religious motives.

Homosexuality = Sexual attraction to a person of the same gender.

Hosanna = 'Save us!' – the greeting of the crowd as Jesus entered Jerusalem.

Human rights = The basic entitlements of every person on the planet.

Human trafficking = The transportation of human beings from one country to another for the purposes of exploitation.

Humanae Vitae: On Human Life = A famous letter written by the Pope in 1968 which confirmed the traditional Catholic teaching.

Hymns = The traditional term for songs sung during worship.

Iconoclasm = The smashing up of religious art or statues.

Icthus = The famous 'fish' symbol for Jesus.

Id-ul-Adha = Festival of Ibrahim's Sacrifice.

Id-al-Fitr = Festival at the end of *Ramadān*.

Idolatry = Worshipping an image, person or anything which is not God.

Imago Dei = Latin for 'the image of God'.

Imam (in Sunni Islam) = One who leads prayers in the mosque.

Imam (in Shi'a Islam) = One of the Twelve leaders of Islam who were descendants and successors of Muhammad.

Immanent = God is present to all creation.

Immanent Trinity = God's innermost being, the inner life of the Triune God.

Incarnate Son = Jesus is God's love enfleshed in a human life.

Incarnation = God becoming human in Jesus.

Ineffable = Means 'indescribable, unutterable, beyond description'.

Infallible = 'Indisputable' pronouncements made by a pope in the name of the Church.

Inspired = 'God breathed' – writings bearing the mark of God.

Isaiah = Prophet of the Old Testament.

Israfil = The Angel of Healing.

Jannah = Eternal paradise.

Jibril = The Angel of Revelation.

Jihad = A term used for Islamic holy war.

> **Greater** *Jihad* = The inner struggle to conquer temptation and live as a good Muslim.

> **Lesser** *Jihad* = The outer struggle to defend the cause of Islam and the *ummah*.

Jinn = spirit beings.

Judgement = An action whereby God determines your fate.

Jummah **Prayer** = The Friday community prayers.

Just war = A war that is morally right.

Kaddish = A hymn of praise to God said at the end of Shabbat services.

Kapels = Skullcaps.

Keriah = Tearing of clothes in mourning.

Kesher echad = One unit, or one bond.

Ketubah = Marriage contract.

Ketuvim = Writings.

Khums = One-fifth or 20% of certain items which a person acquires as wealth, and which must be paid as an Islamic tax.

Kiddush = Blessing said over wine.

Kiddushin = Marriage blessing.

Kingdom of God = The central message of Jesus' preaching.

Kinyan = Acquisition (gaining something).

Kippah = A skullcap worn by Jewish men or boys.

Kol Nidrei = All the vows.

Kosher = Proper or correct.

Laity/Laypeople = From the Greek for 'people' – the baptised people of God, members of the Body of Christ.

Lamb of God = A title given to Jesus in the Gospels.

Last Rites = The sacraments which are often received just before death: confession, communion and anointing of the sick.

Laylat al-Qadr = Night of Power.

Lectern = A reading stand from which the scriptures are proclaimed.

Lechem Cherut = Bread of freedom.

Lectionary = A book containing Bible readings divided according to the calendar of festivals and seasons.

Liberation theology = A Catholic movement dedicated to the preferential option for the poor.

Literary forms = Types of writing such as law, history and prophecy.

Lumen Gentium = Literally, 'light of the nations' – an important document on the Church from the Second Vatican Council.

Ma'ariv = Evening.

Mahdi = A ruler who heralds the Day of Judgement.

Magen David = Star of David.

Magisterium = Teaching authority of the Catholic Church.

Magnificat = The Song of Mary from Luke 1:46–55.

malā'ikah = Angel/messenger.

Malachi = Prophet of the Old Testament.

Martyr = From the Greek word meaning 'witness'.

Martyrdom = Literally 'to give witness' but now usually associated with giving one's life for a cause.

Mass setting = Music which accompanies the *acclamations* of the Mass. Not the same as: **Hymns**.

Mechitzah = A screen used usually to separate men and women in a synagogue.

Menorah = A seven-branched candlestick.

Mercy = God is forgiving.

Messiah = 'Anointed One' in Hebrew.

Messianic secret = The reluctance of Jesus to be openly identified as the Messiah.

Mezuzah = A parchment with religious texts and attached in a cylindrical case to the doorpost of a Jewish house as a sign of faith.

Michelangelo = Italian artist who lived from 1475 to 1564.

Midrash = Teachings from the Rabbis (Rabbinic teachings).

Mikveh = Ritual bath – used for purification rites.

Mika'il = The Angel of Mercy.

Milah = Cutting/Circumcision.

Mincha = Afternoon.

Miracle = An extraordinary occurrence attributed to the action of God.

Mishnah = The collection of sayings from the Oral Law.

Mitzvah = Commandment.

Mitzvot = Commandments.

Mizrach = The wall facing Jerusalem.

Mohel = Jewish man who performs *Brit Milah*.

Monogram = A symbol made up of letters.

Monotheism = Belief in one God.

Mosque – *al-masjid* = 'Place of worship' or 'prostration'.

Mother Julian of Norwich = A Christian mystic from the Middle Ages.

Mount Sinai = The mountain where God gave the Ten Commandments to Moses.

Muktzeh = Objects that are not useable during Shabbat.

Natural family planning = When couples engage in sexual intimacy according to a fertility cycle.

Natural Law = Rules for living which are observable from nature.

Ne'ilah = Sealing or closing.

Ner Tamid = Ever-burning light.

Nevi'im = Prophets.

New Testament = Writings on God and humanity understood through Jesus and the apostles.

Niāb = The minimum amount to be given.

Nicene Creed = This creed was first formulated at Nicaea in AD 325 and was completed in AD 381 at the Council of Constantinople, and it is used in Christian Churches to the present day.

Nidation = The nestling of the fertilised egg in the womb.

Nuclear family = Husband and wife and children.

Nuclear weapons = The most powerful WMD.

Old Testament = Writings on God and humanity understood through the people of Israel.

Olam Ha-Ba = Hebrew word meaning the spiritual afterlife.

Omnipotent = 'All powerful'.

Onan = The person who is in charge of the funeral preparations.

Pacifism = The idea that all warfare is wrong.

Palm Sunday = Christian celebration of Jesus' entry into Jerusalem.

Paralysed = Unable to move arms, legs or both.

Parev = Non-meat or dairy food such as eggs, vegetables, fruit, cereals, beans and fish.

Paschal candle = The Easter symbol of Christ's resurrection in Catholic churches.

Paschal Mystery = This comes from the Hebrew *Pesach* – meaning Passover.

Passover = The Jewish feast of liberation from Egypt.

Passover lamb = The ritual sacrifice made at Passover

Patriarchs = A name for the ancient forefathers of Judaism, such as Abraham, Isaac and Jacob.

Pentecost = Comes from '50' and was a special harvest feast which took place fifty days after Passover and commemorated the giving of the Law to Moses.

Pentateuch = The first five books of the Torah – namely, Genesis, Exodus, Leviticus, Deuteronomy and Numbers.

Perichoresis = A Greek word which tries to describe God's inner life as an eternal interplay of mutual love.

Pesach = Passover.

Peter = A name meaning 'rock' – the leader of the apostles.

Philia = Friendship love.

Pidyon ha-Ben = Redemption of the firstborn.

Pikuach nefesh = Saving a life.

Pilate = Governor of the Roman province of Judea from 26 to 37 CE.

Pilgrim People of God =

A description of the members of the Church.

Pilgrimage = A prayerful journey to a holy place.

Pontifical = To do with the Pope (or 'pontiff').

Prayer = The raising of one's mind and heart to God, consciously making time to be with God, to remember that all of life is lived in God's presence.

Prayer posture = Physical expression of a prayerful disposition. Some common postures are standing, kneeling, prostration and sitting.

Preferential option for the poor = A motto which guides Catholic practice in the face of poverty

Prejudice = An unjustified negative attitude towards an individual or group.

Premarital sex = Intercourse before marriage.

Promiscuity = Sexually irresponsible behaviour.

Prophet = Someone who speaks God's word.

Purgatory = A place of preparation for eternal communion with God.

Qur'ān = The Holy Book of Islam.

Rabbi = Teacher or Master.

Rabbis = Leaders and teachers of Jewish faith and tradition.

Radicalisation = The process whereby ordinary people become extremists in thought and deed.

Rak'ahs = A sequence of movements in prayer.

Ramadān = The Islamic month of fasting.

Rasūl = Messenger.

Real Presence = The Catholic and Orthodox belief that Christ is sacramentally present in the consecrated bread and wine of the Eucharist.

Reacha = 'Neighbour' or 'Friend'.

Rebus = A coded symbol.

Recapitulation = A redemption theory associated with St Irenaeus.

Racism = Prejudice against someone because of their nationality, ethnic origin or culture.

Reconciliation = The restoration of friendly relations.

Reconstituted family = When one or both partners have been married.

Redemption = The way in which Jesus has reconciled humanity to God – sometimes referred to as **salvation** or **atonement**.

Refugees = People fleeing their country because of war, persecution or natural disaster.

Remarriage = The wedding of someone whose first marriage was annulled.

Repentance = Recognising your sin and turning towards God, seeking his mercy.

Restorative Justice = A system of criminal justice which focuses on the rehabilitation of offenders through reconciliation with victims and the community at large.

Resurrection = In Judaism, the belief that the dead arise on Judgement Day.

Risalah = The Message.

Righteous anger = Anger which springs from an objective sense of injustice.

Rosh Hashanah = Head of the Year.

Sabbath = The seventh and holiest day of the Jewish week.

Sacrament = A visible and effective sign of God's invisible grace.

Sacrament of Reconciliation = Sacrament in which a Catholic confesses sins to a priest and is reconciled to God and the Church.

Sacred music = Music and song that is written to honour God.

Sacrifice of the Mass = The Catholic and Orthodox belief that the Mass both commemorates and re-presents the mystery of redemption.

Sadaqah = Voluntary almsgiving.

Salah = Daily prayer.

Salvation = God's rescuing of humanity from sin.

Same-sex marriage = The legally binding civil commitment of a homosexual couple to each other.

Same-sex families = Where the couple (in a legal marriage or civil partnership, or cohabiting) are the same sex. Children may be adopted, or be from a previous relationship, from a surrogate mother or from a sperm donation.

Sanctity of life = Life is holy and belongs to God.

Sanhedrin = The Jewish governing council.

Satan = The spiritual being who is opposed to the goodness of God.

Satisfaction = A redemption theory associated with St Anselm.

Sawm = Fasting.

Scribe = Writer of the *Torah* scroll and repairer of scrolls.

Scripture = The inspired collection of writings called the Bible.

Scripture Bible = An *inspired* collection of writings sacred to Christians.

Seder = Order.

Sefer Torah = Torah scrolls.

Sex = From the Latin sectare – 'to cut', 'divide' or 'separate' – the *different* condition of humans as male or female.

Sexual Intercourse Marital = Connected to marriage.

Sexual Intercourse Procreative = leading to human offspring.

Sexual Intercourse Unitive = Leading to deeper intimacy.

Shadchan = Matchmaker.

Shekhinah = God's divine presence (see Exodus 25:8).

Sh'vut = Lesser prohibitions for people during Shabbat.

Shabbat = The Jewish Sabbath. A day of rest.

Shacharit = Early morning.

Shalom = Peace.

Shalom Bat = Ritual greeting of a newborn daughter.

Shalom Zachar = Ritual greeting of a newborn son.

Shahadah = 'There is no God but Allah and Muhammad is his messenger'.

Shechitah = The humane way of slaughtering animals according to Jewish law.

Sheloshim = A period of 30 days after a burial.

Shema = The main declaration of Jewish faith.

Sheol = A place of the dead awaiting purification.

Sheva Berachot = Seven marriage blessings.

Shirk = Idolatry; worship other than of God.

Shiva = Seven.

Shochet = An officially certified person who slaughters cattle and poultry in accordance with Jewish law.

Shofar = A ram's horn trumpet used in Jewish religious ceremonies.

Siddur = A book of the order of service and prayer for synagogue worship.

Signs/symbols = Material things (i.e. things we can see, touch, hear, taste or smell) that point to spiritual things.

Single-parent family = Where one parent brings up the children alone.

Socialism = The distribution of wealth is based on free markets but moderated by the government.

Sofer = Jewish scribe.

Solidarity = Acting together in a common cause.

Son of God = Jesus is divine, Son of the Father.

Son of Man = Jesus is human, Son of Mary.

Soul = The divine essence of a human being.

Stations of the Cross = A prayer based on the crucifixion of Jesus.

Stewardship = Recognising that everything we have is a gift from God for all humanity and treating it as such.

Sunni and Shi'a = The two main branches of Islam.

Surah = A chapter in the Qur'ān.

Sustainability = Help which makes people independent and is not wasteful of resources.

Symbol = Literally 'put together' – a sign with a connected meaning.

Synagogue = The place of worship for Jews.

Tabernacle = An ornate cabinet in which the Blessed Sacrament is reserved.

Tachrichim = A simple white shroud used to dress a corpse.

Tallit = Prayer shawl usually worn by men.

Talmud = The oral law in Judaism.

Tawhīd = The oneness of God.

Tawāf = The circling of the Ka'aba.

Tefillin = Two black leather boxes for prayer strapped on the head and the arm, worn by Jewish males.

Tenakh = Hebrew Bible: *Law, Prophets, Writings*.

Terrorism = Indiscriminate violence on behalf of a cause.

Teshuvah = A month of repentance.

The Crusades = A Christian holy war.

The Lord's Prayer/Our Father = The prayer Jesus taught his disciples.

The Resurrection = The bodily rising of Jesus from the dead on Easter day.

Theology of the Body = A series of reflections by pope St John Paul II on human sexuality.

Tishri = A Jewish month which usually occurs during September or October.

Torah = The Hebrew word for Law.

Torture = The specific use of violence to extract information or as a means of revenge.

Totus tuus = Latin for 'Totally yours' or 'All I am is yours'.

Tradition = The *inspired wisdom* captured in the words, customs and lives of Christians.

Transcendent = God is beyond all creation.

Transfiguration = The glory of God shining in Jesus.

Transubstantiation = A way of explaining how Christ is present in the Eucharist under the appearance of bread and wine.

Trefah = Forbidden.

Trinity/Triune = The teaching of the Church that the nature of God is one and three.

Trinity = God understood as Father – Son – Spirit in the Christian revelation.

Twelve = Name given to the apostles.

Types of prayer = Adoration, thanksgiving, repentance, intercession, petition.

Tzavta = Connection or binding.

Tzedakah = Giving to charity.

Universal destination of goods = God destined the earth and all its resources for all people.

Utilitarianism = This is a non-religious world view which says that moral choice should maximise pleasure and minimise pain.

Ummah = The worldwide community of Muslims.

Uvdin D'chol = Weekday tasks.

Umrah = A lesser pilgrimage.

Unleavened bread = The special bread eaten during Passover.

Veil of the Temple = A veil or curtain in a Temple that separated the Holy of Holies – the earthly dwelling place of God's presence – from the rest of the Temple where men dwelt.

Valid Marriage = A marriage recognised by the Catholic Church.

Violence = Hurtful physical actions towards another.

Virtue = A desirable moral quality.

Vocation = From the Latin for 'calling'.

Weibershul = An upstairs gallery for women in some orthodox synagogues.

Words of Institution = The words of Jesus at the Last Supper offering the bread and wine to the disciples – 'This is my body, this is my blood, do this in memory of me.'

Wudu = Ritual washing.

Wilderness = The dry desert area in the south-east of Israel/Palestine.

WMD = Weapons of Mass Destruction – armaments which can devastate large areas and kill many people.

Yad = A pointer to read the Torah with.

Yahrzeit = Death anniversary.

YHWH = Hebrew name for God.

Yichad = Private room for newlyweds.

Yom Kippur = Jewish Day of Atonement (reconciliation between humans and God).

Zakah = Charitable giving.

Author Biographies

Anthony Towey, PhD. is Director in the Aquinas Centre for Catholic Education at St Mary's University. Anthony was Head of RE in Manchester before joining Strawberry Hill in 2005. He has worked in liaison with NIBRIA and Catholic HEIs to ensure the theological integrity of the Specifications for AQA. Anthony is joint editor of the textbook with a particular focus on the Catholic component.

Philip Robinson, M.Phil is Religious Education Advisor to the CES (Catholic Education Service), former Head of RE and Diocesan Advisor in the Diocese of Hexam and Newcastle, and consultant on the design of the Specification and its assessment matrix. He is joint editor of this textbook and has helped ensure its suitability for pupils and teachers in Catholic schools seeking to study and work towards GCSE RE examination success.

George Skelton M.A. has taught RE at all key stages of secondary level for over 30 years. He is currently at Holy Family Catholic School, Walthamstow and has brought his vast experience to bear particularly on the sections dealing with Mark's Gospel.

Shelley Victor M.Th. is a graduate of religious studies and currently head of RE at Gumley House Convent School, Isleworth. An exponent of clarity and organisation in the classroom, Shelley has made a particular contribution to the section on Judaism.

Duncan MacPherson PhD. is an emeritus fellow of St Mary's University, Twickenham, where he taught Religious Studies and trained students for teaching over many years. Duncan has contributed specifically to the section on Islam.

Ben Gray M.A. Currently teaches Religious Studies at Worth Abbey School and is former Head of Department at St Winifred's Catholic School, Crawley. Ben is an innovative teacher and has contributed most specifically to RE themes such as relationships and global issues.

Text by

Anthony Towey

Philip Robinson

George Skelton

Shelley Victor

Duncan MacPherson

Ben Gray

Edited by

Anthony Towey

Additional contributors

Kathleen O'Brien

Paul Rowan